DOMINATING CLIENT
ONBOARDING

BOOK 3

The Path to Prosperity Series

STRATEGIC ADVISOR BOARD
ACHIEVE SYSTEMS PRO

ISBN: 978-1-957217-71-0 (hardcover)
ISBN: 978-1-957217-72-7 (paperback)
ISBN: 978-1-957217-73-4 (ebook)

TABLE OF CONTENTS

Introduction v

Chapter 1: The Importance of Client Engagement 1

Chapter 2: The Onboarding Process 9

Chapter 3: Sustaining Engagement Through
            Communication 20

Chapter 4: Content as Currency 29

Chapter 5: Extending Engagement to Fulfillment 38

Chapter 6: Capitalizing on Auto Payments 48

Chapter 7: Case Study: Evergood Adventure Wines. . . . 58

Chapter 8: Best Practices for Sustainable Engagement. . . 68

Chapter 9: Metrics and Measurement 81

Chapter 10: Conclusion 96

INTRODUCTION

In today's dynamic business landscape, acquiring clients is only the first step toward sustainable success. The true challenge lies in retaining their interest and fostering long-term relationships. As markets become increasingly competitive and consumer preferences evolve rapidly, the need to keep clients engaged throughout their journey with your business has never been more crucial.

Imagine this: You've successfully onboarded a client, but then what? How do you ensure they remain invested in your products or services? How do you prevent them from seeking alternatives or drifting away into oblivion? This book is your guide to navigating these challenges and mastering the art of client engagement.

Every interaction matters from the moment a prospect enters your ecosystem to the final stage of fulfillment. Each touchpoint presents an opportunity to deepen the relationship, provide value, and ultimately drive revenue. Businesses can transform one-time buyers into loyal advocates through strategic communication, compelling content, and seamless experiences.

Drawing on real-world examples, proven strategies, and expert insights, this book offers a comprehensive roadmap for enhancing client engagement. Whether you're a seasoned entrepreneur or a budding startup, the principles outlined here will empower you to build lasting connections, maximize customer lifetime value, and thrive in an ever-evolving marketplace.

Join us as we explore the pivotal role of client engagement in today's business landscape and uncover actionable tactics for cultivating meaningful relationships that stand the test of time.

In the fast-paced business world, where trends shift and technologies evolve at breakneck speed, one truth remains constant: the importance of client engagement. In an era of fierce competition and consumer expectations are higher than ever, simply acquiring clients is no longer enough to ensure success. The real challenge lies in keeping them engaged, satisfied, and loyal over the long term.

Client engagement is not just a buzzword or a passing trend; it's a fundamental aspect of modern business strategy. It's about building relationships, fostering trust, and delivering value at every touchpoint along the customer journey. From the initial onboarding process to post-purchase interactions and beyond, every interaction with a client is an opportunity to deepen the relationship and create a loyal advocate for your brand.

This book will explore the various facets of client engagement and provide practical strategies and actionable insights to help you master this essential skill. Drawing on real-world examples from diverse industries, we will examine the key principles and best practices for keeping clients engaged and satisfied throughout their journey with your business.

We will delve into the power of strategic communication, the importance of compelling content, and the value of creating seamless and memorable experiences for your clients. We will also explore the role of data analytics in understanding client behavior and tailoring your engagement strategies to meet their needs effectively.

Whether you're a seasoned entrepreneur looking to fine-tune your client engagement efforts or a budding startup eager to make a lasting impression on your clients, this book is for you. Our goal is simple: to provide you with the knowledge, tools, and inspiration you need to build meaningful relationships with your clients and drive sustainable growth for your business.

Join us as we embark on this journey together. Let's unlock the secrets to successful client engagement and pave the way for a future filled with loyal and satisfied customers.

1

THE IMPORTANCE OF CLIENT ENGAGEMENT

As a business owner, I know keeping my customers happy isn't just about making a sale. It's about building relationships that last. That's where client engagement comes in. But what exactly is client engagement, and why does it matter?

Client engagement is all about how well you connect with your customers. It's not just about selling them something; it's about making them feel valued and involved in what you do. Building these connections is more important than ever in today's fast-paced world, where customers have plenty of options.

Think about it this way: If you only focus on making a sale, you're missing out on the bigger picture. Sure, you might make some money in the short term, but what about the long term? Building lasting relationships with your customers keeps them returning for more. It's what turns them into loyal supporters of your business.

That's why it's crucial to move beyond just transactional relationships. Making a sale is important, but it's only the beginning. To succeed in business, you must foster long-term connections with your customers. You need to make them feel like they're part of something bigger than just a one-time purchase.

In this chapter, we'll dive deep into client engagement. We'll explore what it means, why it's important, and how you can use it to drive success in your business. So, buckle up because we're about to embark on a journey to discover the power of client engagement.

THE EVOLVING BUSINESS LANDSCAPE

Running a business isn't like it used to be. These days, things are always changing, especially when it comes to how people buy stuff. Customers aren't just looking for a product anymore. They want an experience, and that's where things get tricky.

Back in the day, you could slap a price tag on something and call it a day. Now, customers expect more. They want to feel like they're part of something special. They want to be wowed, impressed, and treated like VIPs.

With all this competition out there, standing out isn't easy. Many businesses are vying for your customer's attention, all trying to outdo each other with flashy ads and fancy gimmicks. It's like a never-ending battle to be the coolest kid on the block.

However, here's the thing: In today's world, being cool isn't enough. You've got to be more than just a pretty face. You've got to connect with your customers on a deeper level. You've got to give them an experience they won't forget.

That's where the "experience economy" comes in. It's all about creating moments that matter and leave a lasting impression on your customers. It's about turning a simple transaction into something magical, something they'll tell their friends about for weeks to come.

Pulling off this whole experience thing isn't easy. It takes time, effort, and a whole lot of creativity. You've got to think outside the box, try new things, and constantly adapt to changing trends.

In this chapter, we will take a closer look at how the business landscape is evolving. We'll explore how customer behavior is changing, why competition is fiercer than ever, and what it all means for your business. So, get ready to roll up your sleeves and dive into the world of the experience economy. It will be a wild ride, but trust me, it'll be worth it.

BUILDING TRUST AND LOYALTY

Let's talk about trust and loyalty—two things every business owner wants from their customers. And you know what? Client engagement is the secret sauce that makes it all happen.

When you engage with your customers, you're not just selling them something—you're building a relationship. You're showing them that you care about more than just making a buck. You're showing them that you're in it for the long haul.

When you build that trust with your customers, something magical happens. They keep coming back for more. They tell their friends about you. They become your biggest fans.

That's because satisfied customers are loyal customers. When you go above and beyond to make them happy, they reward you with loyalty. And that loyalty? Well, it's worth its weight in gold.

However, don't just take my word for it. Let's look at some real-life examples. Take Apple, for instance. They don't just sell phones and computers—they sell a lifestyle. They engage with their customers in a way that makes them feel like they're part of something bigger than just a product.

3

Or how about Starbucks? They've built an empire on more than just coffee. They've built a community that keeps people coming back day after day.

And then there's Amazon. They've mastered the art of client engagement like no other. From personalized recommendations to lightning-fast shipping, they've set the bar high for what it means to keep customers happy.

So, what's the takeaway? It's simple: When you engage with your customers, you build trust. And when you build trust, you build loyalty. And when you build loyalty, well, the sky's the limit. So, get out there and start engaging with your customers. You'll be amazed at what it can do for your business.

Enhancing Customer Lifetime Value

Customer lifetime value, or CLV for short, is super important for any business. You might be thinking, *What the heck is CLV, and why should I care?* Well, let me break it down for you.

CLV is all about how much money a customer is worth to your business over the long haul. It's not just about how much they spend in one transaction—it's about how much they'll spend over their entire relationship with you. And trust me, that's a big deal.

When you understand the CLV of your customers, you can make smarter decisions about how you spend your time and money. You can focus on the customers who are most likely to stick around and keep coming back for more. And that, my friend, is the key to sustainable growth.

Now, here's where client engagement comes into play. When you engage with your customers regularly, you're not just building trust and loyalty—you're also increasing their CLV. Think about it: the more connected your customers feel to your business, the more likely they will keep coming back for more.

How can you maximize CLV through client engagement? It's all about staying in touch and building relationships. Send them personalized emails, offer special deals, and show them you care about their needs. Keeping them engaged and happy will ensure they stick around for the long haul.

And don't forget about relationship-building. Take the time to get to know your customers on a personal level. Show them that you're more than just a faceless corporation—you're a friend who's always there to help.

CLV is the name of the game when it comes to business growth. And client engagement? Well, it's the secret weapon that'll help you maximize it. Get out there and start engaging with your customers. Your bottom line will thank you for it.

MITIGATING CHURN AND INCREASING RETENTION

Churn is just a fancy word for losing customers. And let me tell you, it's the last thing any business owner wants to deal with. It's bad news for your bottom line when customers start jumping ship. That's why it's crucial to understand what churn is all about and how you can stop it in its tracks.

Churn happens when customers decide to take their business elsewhere. Maybe they found a better deal, or maybe they just got tired of what you're offering. Whatever the reason, it's a problem. And if you're not careful, it can sink your business faster than you can say, "Uh-oh."

Client engagement can be your secret weapon against churn. Keeping your customers engaged and happy makes them less likely to look for greener pastures. It's all about building those relationships and making them feel like they're part of something special.

How do you do it? Well, first off, you've got to stay in touch. Send them regular emails, give them special deals, and show them that you care about their needs. And don't just wait for them to come to you—be proactive. Reach out to them when you haven't heard from them in a while, and make sure they know you're there to help.

However, it's not just about staying in touch. You've also got to get to the bottom of why customers are leaving in the first place. Maybe they're unhappy with your product or service, or maybe they're just not feeling valued. Whatever the reason, it's up to you to figure it out and address it head-on.

Churn is the enemy of every business owner. However, with the power of client engagement on your side, you can keep those customers coming back for more.

Competitive Advantage through Client Engagement

Next, let's talk about standing out in a sea of competitors—because, trust me, it's tough out there. However, client engagement can be your secret weapon when it comes to gaining a competitive edge.

When you engage with your customers in a meaningful way, you're not just selling them a product or service. You're building a connection that sets you apart from the competition. And that, my friend, is worth its weight in gold.

In today's crowded marketplace, customers have plenty of options. They can choose from a million different businesses, all offering pretty much the same thing. So, how do you make them choose you?

The answer lies in how well you engage with your customers. When you go above and beyond to make them feel valued and appreciated, you're not just selling them a product—you're selling them an experience. And that's something your competitors can't replicate.

However, it's not just about making your customers feel warm and fuzzy inside. It's also about giving them a reason to choose you over the competition. Maybe it's your top-notch customer service, lightning-fast shipping, or killer loyalty program. Whatever it is, it's what sets you apart from the pack.

And you know what? It works. Just look at companies like Zappos, Southwest Airlines, and Chick-fil-A. They've built empires on the back of stellar client engagement. They've turned their customers into raving fans who wouldn't dream of going elsewhere.

Client engagement isn't just a nice-to-have—it's a must-have. It sets you apart from the competition and gives you a fighting chance in today's cutthroat marketplace.

CONCLUSION

In this chapter, we've talked about the importance of client engagement and how it's not just about making sales—it's about building lasting relationships. We've explored how engaging with your customers can help you stand out in a crowded marketplace and give you a competitive edge. We've also seen how businesses like Zappos and Chick-fil-A have used client engagement to become industry leaders.

Client engagement is essential for your business's success. When you engage with your customers in a meaningful way, you build trust, loyalty, and a loyal customer base. And that, my friend, is worth its weight in gold.

In the chapters to come, we'll be diving into practical strategies for enhancing client engagement. We'll explore things like email marketing, social media, and customer loyalty programs. We'll also examine data analytics and how it can help you better understand your customers' needs.

We're about to take your client engagement game to the next level. Trust me, it will be a wild ride, but I promise it'll be worth it in the end. Stick around, and let's make some magic happen together.

2

THE ONBOARDING PROCESS

You might be wondering, *What the heck is onboarding, and why should I care?* Well, let me break it down for you. Onboarding is all about welcoming new customers into the fold. It's like rolling out the red carpet and saying, "Hey, we're glad you're here!" But it's more than just a warm welcome—it's the foundation for a great customer experience.

When you onboard a new customer the right way, you're setting the stage for success. You show them you're organized, attentive, and ready to meet their needs. And trust me, that's a big deal.

When you buy something new, whether a product or a service, you want to feel like you made the right choice. You want to feel confident that you made a smart decision. And that's where onboarding comes in.

However, not all onboarding experiences are created equal. Some are smooth sailing, while others are, well, a bit rough around the edges. And that can make all the difference when it comes to keeping customers happy and coming back for more.

In this chapter, we'll take a closer look at what makes a great onboarding experience tick. We'll explore the key components and strategies that go into creating a seamless onboarding process. Let's get started!

UNDERSTANDING THE CUSTOMER JOURNEY

The customer journey is like a road trip—from the moment someone hears about your business to the point where they become a loyal customer. It's a journey with twists, turns, and sometimes a few bumps along the way.

First is the prospect stage. This is where someone hears about your business for the first time—maybe through an ad, a friend's recommendation, or a Google search. They're curious, but they're not committed yet. It's like they're window-shopping, checking things out from a distance.

Next comes the consideration stage. This is where things start to get serious. The prospect is thinking, *Hmm, maybe this business is worth a closer look.* They're doing their research, comparing options, and weighing the pros and cons. It's like they're kicking the tires, trying to decide if your business is the right fit for them.

Then, we've got the decision stage. This is where the rubber meets the road. The prospect has done their homework, and now they're ready to decide. They're reaching for their wallet, ready to take the plunge and become a customer. It's like they're stepping up to the checkout counter, credit card in hand.

However, the journey doesn't end there. Once someone becomes a customer, the real work begins. That's where onboarding comes in. It's all about making sure that first-time customers have a smooth and seamless experience from start to finish.

Onboarding isn't always smooth sailing. Sometimes, there are hiccups, bumps in the road, and frustrations along the way. Maybe the signup process is confusing, or the product doesn't work as expected. These are the common challenges and pain points customers face during the onboarding process.

So, why is it important to map out the customer journey and identify these touchpoints? Well, it's simple. By understanding where customers are coming from, what they're looking for, and where they might hit roadblocks, you can create a better onboarding experience. You can smooth out the bumps, address their concerns, and guide them along the path to becoming loyal customers. And that, my friend, is what it's all about.

DESIGNING A SEAMLESS ONBOARDING EXPERIENCE

Let's talk about creating a killer onboarding experience for your customers. Trust me, it's a game-changer when it comes to keeping them happy and coming back for more.

First, I want to discuss the importance of keeping things simple. When it comes to onboarding, less is more. You want to ensure the process is as user-friendly and intuitive as possible. That means no confusing forms, no jargon-filled instructions— just a smooth and seamless experience from start to finish.

How do you do it? It's all about simplifying and streamlining the process. Think about it like this: You wouldn't build a maze for your customers to navigate, would you? Of course not! You'd give them a clear path from point A to point B, with no obstacles in their way.

That's where strategies like using clear and concise language, minimizing the number of steps involved, and providing helpful guidance along the way come into play. You want to make it as easy as possible for your customers to get up and running without breaking a sweat.

A user-friendly onboarding process is just the beginning. To really knock it out of the park, you've got to add a personal touch. You want your customers to feel like they're more than just a number—they're valued members of your community.

That's where personalized touches come in. Maybe it's a welcome email with their name on it or a personalized video message from you, the business owner. Whatever it is, it's all about making your customers feel seen, heard, and appreciated.

When it comes to onboarding, simplicity and personalization are the names of the game. Keep things easy, make your customers feel special, and watch as they become your biggest fans.

Communicating Value Propositions

Communicating the value of what we offer during the onboarding process is crucial to our business success. This is where we make sure our customers know exactly why our product or service is worth their time and money.

First, we need to articulate our unique value propositions. That's just a fancy way of saying what makes us special. Maybe it's our lightning-fast delivery, top-notch customer service, or unbeatable prices. Whatever it is, we need to make sure our customers know about it from the get-go.

However, it's not enough to just shout our value propositions from the rooftops. We have to do it in a way that resonates with our customers. That means speaking their language, addressing their needs, and solving their pain points.

So, how do we do it? It's all about effective communication. We must ensure our messaging is clear, concise, and compelling. There is no jargon or fluff—just straight talk that gets the job done.

But here's the kicker: It's not just about what we say—it's also about how we say it. We need to meet our customers where they are, whether through email, social media, or face-to-face interactions. And we need to make sure our messaging is consistent across all channels, so our customers know exactly what to expect.

Perhaps most importantly, we need to make sure our value propositions align with our customers' expectations. That means delivering on our promises every single time. If we say we offer fast shipping, we better deliver those packages on time. If we say we offer 24/7 support, we better be there when our customers need us.

We build trust and credibility when our value propositions align with our customers' expectations. Therefore, let's ensure we communicate our value propositions loud and clear. Then, let's deliver on them like nobody's business.

PROVIDING EDUCATIONAL RESOURCES

Another important aspect of business is customer education. Customers can make smarter decisions when they know more about our products or services. And that's good for everyone involved.

When you buy a new gadget, don't you want to know how it works? Of course you do! That's why providing educational resources is so important. It helps our customers understand what they're getting and how to get the most out of it.

However, educating our customers isn't just about throwing a bunch of information at them and hoping for the best. It's about delivering that information in a way that's engaging and easy to understand.

There are many ways to do this. We can create tutorials that walk our customers through the ins and outs of our products or services. We can write guides that answer common questions and address common concerns. And we can even host webinars where our customers can ask questions and get answers in real time.

But here's where it gets exciting: We can incorporate interactive elements to make the learning experience even more engaging. That means quizzes, polls, videos—you name it.

The goal is to keep our customers interested and involved every step of the way.

When our customers feel empowered to make informed decisions, they will likely stick around. They're more likely to become loyal customers who come back to us time and time again.

ESTABLISHING CLEAR EXPECTATIONS

Next, let's talk about setting clear expectations with our customers. When we're onboarding someone new, it's important to lay all our cards on the table from the get-go.

When you buy something, you want to know what you're getting, right? You don't want any surprises or hidden fees popping up down the road. That's why setting clear expectations is so important.

How do we do it? First, we need to be upfront about our product features, pricing, and support. That means giving our customers all the information they need to make an informed decision. No fine print, no bait and switch—just straight talk.

But here's the thing: sometimes things don't go according to plan. Maybe our product doesn't work as expected, or our customer support isn't up to snuff. That's where managing customer expectations comes in. We must proactively address potential concerns or misunderstandings before they become big problems.

So, how do we do that? It's all about communication. We need to keep our customers in the loop every step of the way. If there's a shipping delay or a glitch in our system, we need to let them know immediately. And we need to be honest about what went wrong and how we will fix it.

Transparent communication builds trust and credibility with our customers. When they know they can count on us to be honest and upfront, they're more likely to stick around— even when things don't go perfectly. Overall, setting clear expectations with our customers from day one is vital. This includes being upfront about what we offer and being proactive about addressing any concerns or misunderstandings that come up along the way.

PERSONALIZED ONBOARDING JOURNEYS

Let's talk about personalized onboarding journeys—because when it comes to making our customers feel special, this is where the magic happens.

Every customer is different. They all have their individual needs, preferences, and quirks. And if we want to keep them happy, we've got to tailor their onboarding experience to fit like a glove.

But why is this so important? Think about it like this: When you walk into a store and the salesperson remembers your name, asks about your family, and suggests products they know you'll love, how does that make you feel? Pretty darn good, right? That's the power of personalization.

Here's how to do it. First, we need to segment our customers based on things like demographics, behavior, and preferences. That means grouping them into categories—like age, location, or buying habits—and tailoring our onboarding process to each group's unique needs.

Next is the exciting part. We can use automation and data analytics to take our personalization game to the next level. That means using software to track our customers' interactions with our business, analyze their behavior, and deliver personalized experiences at scale.

For example, let's say we have a customer who's always buying our high-end products. We can use that information to send them personalized recommendations for similar products they might like. Or let's say we've got a customer who's struggling to get started with our software. We can send them a series of step-by-step tutorials to help them out.

The possibilities are endless. And the best part? When our customers feel like we're paying attention to their needs and preferences, they're more likely to stick around—and that's good for business.

Measuring Onboarding Success

Regarding our onboarding process's success, it's not enough to just roll out the welcome mat and call it a day. We need to know if our efforts are paying off—and if not, what we can do better.

To do this, we first need to identify some key performance indicators (KPIs). These are basically metrics that tell us how well our onboarding process is working. Maybe it's the number of customers who complete the onboarding process or the time it takes for them to get up and running. Whatever it is, we need to keep an eye on these KPIs to see if we're moving in the right direction.

However, numbers only tell part of the story. That's why it's also important to gather feedback from our customers. We need to know if they're happy with the onboarding experience, if they have any suggestions for improvement, and if there are any pain points we need to address.

There are many ways to gather this feedback. We can send out surveys, host focus groups, or even just pick up the phone and give our customers a call. The important thing is that we're listening to what they have to say and taking their feedback seriously.

Perhaps most importantly, we need to leverage the power of data analytics. Data can tell us a lot about how our customers are interacting with our business. It can tell us which parts of the onboarding process are working well and which parts need improvement. Armed with this information, we can make informed decisions about how to optimize our onboarding process for continuous improvement.

Measuring the success of our onboarding process is all about keeping an eye on our KPIs, gathering customer feedback, and leveraging data analytics to make informed decisions. It's not always easy, but it's worth the effort.

CASE STUDIES AND EXAMPLES

There are many real-world examples of successful onboarding experiences, and sometimes, the best way to learn is by seeing what other folks are doing right. So, let's take a peek at a few shining examples from leading companies across different industries.

The first is Amazon. When you sign up for Amazon Prime, you're not just getting free shipping—you're getting a whole package of perks, from streaming movies and music to exclusive deals. And the onboarding process? It's seamless. They walk you through every step of the way, making sure you know what you're getting and how to make the most of it.

Then, there's Slack. If you've ever used Slack, you know how addictive it can be. However, what sets Slack apart is its onboarding process. They make it super easy to get started, with helpful tutorials and tips popping up along the way. And before you know it, you're hooked.

Let's not forget about Netflix. When you sign up for Netflix, they don't just throw you into the deep end—they take you by the hand and guide you through the process. From personalized recommendations to easy-to-use interfaces, they make sure you feel right at home from day one.

But here's the thing: It's not just about copying what these companies are doing. It's about learning from their successes and applying those lessons to our businesses. Maybe it's taking a page out of Amazon's book and offering a bundle of perks with our product. Or maybe it's borrowing Slack's onboarding approach and ensuring our customers feel supported every step of the way.

The key is to use these real-world examples to inform our onboarding strategies. Because at the end of the day, it's all about creating an experience that keeps our customers coming back for more. And with a little inspiration from the pros, I have no doubt we can do just that.

CONCLUSION

As we wrap up this chapter, let's take a moment to recap what we've covered.

We started by talking about the importance of onboarding—how it's not just about getting customers in the door but about setting the stage for a positive experience that keeps them coming back for more.

Then, we talked about all the different elements that go into a successful onboarding process. We covered everything from clear communication and personalized touches to seamless experiences and setting clear expectations.

Next, we looked at some real-world examples of companies that are knocking it out of the park with their onboarding experiences. From Amazon to Slack to Netflix, we saw how these companies set the bar high and keep their customers happy.

Perhaps most importantly, we talked about why all this matters. A well-executed onboarding process isn't just nice to have—it's essential for driving customer satisfaction and retention. It's what turns one-time buyers into loyal fans who keep coming back for more.

As we move forward, let's keep these key points in mind. Let's ensure our onboarding process is top-notch and keep finding new ways to engage and retain our customers beyond the onboarding phase. Because at the end of the day, happy customers are the key to our success. And with the right strategies in place, I have no doubt we can keep them returning for more.

3

SUSTAINING ENGAGEMENT THROUGH COMMUNICATION

Communication isn't just about sending out messages and hoping for the best. It's about building relationships, fostering trust, and keeping the conversation going.

In this chapter, we will dive into some effective communication strategies that can help us do just that. We'll talk about everything from understanding our customers' communication preferences to creating engaging content that keeps them coming back for more.

We've got a lot to cover. By the time we're done, you'll have a whole toolkit of communication strategies at your disposal. And trust me, your customers are going to love you for it.

UNDERSTANDING CUSTOMER COMMUNICATION PREFERENCES

Different customers have different communication preferences, and every customer is different. Some folks prefer getting emails, while others would rather chat on social media. And if we want to keep them engaged, we've got to speak their language.

That's where understanding their communication preferences comes in. It's about figuring out how they like to be contacted and tailoring our approach accordingly.

To do this, we first need to explore the different communication channels available. These include everything from email and social media to good old-fashioned phone calls.

However, just because a customer prefers one channel over another doesn't mean they want to hear from us all the time. That's where gathering insights comes in. We need to pay attention to how our customers respond to different types of communication and adjust our approach accordingly.

Maybe it's sending out a survey to see which channels they prefer. Or maybe it's tracking their interactions with our business to see which ones they engage with the most.

The key is to listen to our customers and meet them where they're at. Because when we communicate in a way that resonates with them, they're more likely to stick around—and that's good for business.

BUILDING RELATIONSHIPS THROUGH PERSONALIZED COMMUNICATION

Personalized communication is a game-changer when it comes to building strong relationships with our customers.

When someone remembers your name, asks about your interests, and tailors their message just for you, how does that make you feel? Pretty darn special, right? That's the power of personalized communication.

When we take the time to personalize our messages, whether an email, a phone call, or even a handwritten note, it shows our customers we see them as individuals—not just another number on our list.

Personalized communication is all about paying attention to our customers' preferences and behavior. Maybe they always open our emails about a certain topic, or maybe they tend to engage more with us on social media. Whatever it is, we can use that information to tailor our communication to their interests and needs.

But don't just take my word for it—let me share a couple of case studies to illustrate the power of personalized communication.

Take, for example, Sarah's Bakery. They started sending personalized birthday emails to their customers, complete with a special offer just for them. And you know what? It worked like a charm. Not only did it make their customers feel valued, but it also drove a ton of repeat business.

Then, there's Joe's Auto Repair. Instead of sending out generic newsletters, they started sending personalized follow-up emails after each service appointment. They'd include tips for maintaining their car and reminders about upcoming maintenance. And you know what? Their customers loved it. They felt like Joe's really cared about their car—and their safety.

Personalized communication is a must-have for building strong relationships with our customers. And with a little effort and creativity, we can make every one of them feel like a VIP.

CREATING ENGAGING CONTENT

Creating content that keeps our customers coming back for more is all about grabbing their attention and keeping them engaged—and trust me, it's worth the effort.

In today's world, we're bombarded with information left and right. If we want to cut through the noise and capture our customers' attention, we must create content that's not just informative but downright irresistible.

That's where relevance comes in. Our content has to speak directly to our customers' needs, interests, and pain points.

Whether a blog post, social media update, or video tutorial, it has to be something they want to read, watch, or listen to.

However, relevance alone isn't enough. We also have to make sure our content is engaging. That means it must be interesting and entertaining. After all, if our customers are bored, they won't stick around.

Creating engaging content is all about finding the right balance between information and entertainment. Maybe it's incorporating storytelling into our blog posts or adding some eye-catching visuals to our social media updates. Whatever it is, the key is to keep things fresh and engaging.

Take, for example, our recent video tutorial on how to use our product. Instead of just walking through the steps, we added a bit of humor and personality to keep things interesting. And you know what? Our customers loved it.

Or how about our latest blog post, where we shared a behind-the-scenes look at how our product is made? By pulling back the curtain and giving our customers a glimpse into our world, we created a connection that goes beyond just a transaction.

Creating engaging content isn't just about throwing information out into the void—it's about creating meaningful connections with our customers. And with a little creativity and a lot of heart, I have no doubt we can do just that.

LEVERAGING AUTOMATION FOR CONSISTENT COMMUNICATION

Let's talk about automation—specifically, how it can help us keep the lines of communication open with our customers, day in and day out.

You might be thinking, *But won't automation make things feel impersonal?* And hey, I get where you're coming from. However, when done right, automation can make our communication more consistent and personalized than ever before.

With automation, we can set up a series of emails that go out to our customers at just the right time, whether it's to welcome them aboard, follow up after a purchase, or check in on their satisfaction. And because specific actions or events trigger these emails, they feel tailor-made for each customer.

However, it's not just about emails. We can also use automation to power things like chatbots, which can provide instant answers to our customers' questions 24/7. And let me tell you, nothing says "We've got your back," like being able to get help whenever you need it, day or night.

So, how do we do it without sacrificing that personal touch? It's all about finding the right balance. Maybe it's using merge tags to personalize our emails with each customer's name. Or maybe it's setting up rules to ensure our chatbots only kick in when a customer needs help.

The key is to use automation to make our lives easier without losing sight of what's important—keeping our customers happy and engaged. With tools like email marketing platforms and chatbot software at our disposal, I have no doubt we can do just that.

Nurturing Customer Loyalty through Ongoing Communication

Nurturing customer loyalty through ongoing communication is like watering a plant to help it grow. It's not enough to just make a sale and move on. If we want our customers to stick around for the long haul, we have to keep the conversation going, day in and day out.

That's where ongoing communication comes in. It's about staying connected with our customers even after they've made a purchase, whether to check in on their satisfaction, share helpful tips and advice, or just say, "Hey, we're still here for you."

And let me tell you, it's worth the effort. When we stay top-of-mind with our customers, they're more likely to think of us the next time they need something—and that's how we build loyalty.

How do we do it? Well, it's all about finding creative ways to stay connected. Maybe it's sending out a monthly newsletter with helpful tips and updates. Or maybe it's hosting exclusive events or webinars just for our loyal customers.

However, it's not just about communication but also about showing appreciation. That's where loyalty programs and exclusive offers come in. By rewarding our customers for their continued engagement, we're incentivizing them to stick around and showing them that we value their business.

Take, for example, our VIP program. We offer exclusive discounts, early access to new products, and even birthday surprises to our most loyal customers. And let me tell you, they eat it up.

Nurturing customer loyalty through ongoing communication isn't just good business—it's essential. And with a little creativity and a lot of heart, I have no doubt we can keep our customers returning for more, time and time again.

HANDLING CUSTOMER FEEDBACK AND CONCERNS

Handling customer feedback and concerns is a big part of keeping our customers happy and our business thriving. Feedback isn't always easy to hear. But if we want to improve and grow, we must listen to what our customers say, good or bad.

That's where proactive communication comes in. Instead of waiting for our customers to come to us with a problem, we must proactively reach out and ask for their feedback. Whether through surveys, feedback forms, or just picking up the phone and giving them a call, we have to show our customers that we care about what they think.

However, it's not just about collecting feedback—we also must respond to customer feedback effectively. That means acknowledging their concerns, addressing them promptly, and taking action to make things right. When our customers see that we're listening and taking their feedback seriously, it builds trust and loyalty.

Let me share a couple of case studies to illustrate what I'm talking about.

Take, for example, Mary's Boutique. They had a customer who wasn't happy with a dress she ordered online. Instead of ignoring her complaint, they reached out immediately, apologized for the inconvenience, and offered to send her a replacement dress free of charge. Not only did they turn a negative experience into a positive one, but they also won a loyal customer for life.

Then there's John's Tech Store. They had a customer who was frustrated with a glitch in one of their products. Instead of making excuses, they listened to his concerns, investigated the issue, and rolled out a software update to fix the problem. And you know what? That customer stuck around and became an advocate for their brand.

Handling customer feedback and concerns isn't just about putting out fires—it's about building trust and loyalty one conversation at a time. We can turn even the toughest critics into our biggest fans with a proactive approach and a commitment to listening.

MEASURING COMMUNICATION EFFECTIVENESS

Next, let's chat about measuring communication effectiveness—it's like taking a pulse on how well we're connecting with our customers.

Now, you might wonder, *How do we know if our messages are hitting the mark?* That's where metrics come in. These are like little breadcrumbs that tell us if our communication strategies are working or if we need to tweak things a bit.

First, we must identify the right metrics to track. This could be things like open rates for our emails, click-through rates on our website, or even sentiment analysis from customer feedback—anything that gives us insight into how our messages resonate with our audience.

However, it's not just about gathering data—we also must analyze it. That means digging into the numbers to see what's working and what's not. Maybe we notice that our email open rates are higher on Tuesdays or that our customers tend to engage more with video content than written articles. These insights can help us fine-tune our communication strategies for even better results.

That's where analytics tools come in handy. Whether Google Analytics, social media insights, or email marketing platforms, these tools give us the power to track our communication performance in real time. So, if something's not working, we can make adjustments on the fly and course-correct as needed.

Now, I'm not saying it's always easy. Sometimes, the numbers can be overwhelming, and it can feel like we're swimming in a sea of data. However, by staying focused on the metrics that matter most to our business goals, we can stay on track and keep our communication efforts moving in the right direction.

Measuring communication effectiveness isn't just about crunching numbers—it's about using data to fine-tune our messages and strengthen our customer connections. With the right metrics and tools at our disposal, we can keep the conversation going strong.

CONCLUSION

As we wrap up this chapter, let's take a quick look back at what we've covered.

We've discussed the importance of effective communication in keeping our customers engaged and happy. Whether understanding their preferences, personalizing our messages, or handling their feedback with care, communication is the glue that holds our relationships together.

And let me tell you, it's not just about sending out emails or posting on social media—it's about making meaningful connections with our customers, one conversation at a time.

As we move forward, let's remember the lessons we've learned here. Let's keep listening to our customers, responding to their needs, and showing them that we're here for them every step of the way. Effective communication isn't just about talking—it's about building trust, loyalty, and lasting relationships.

With that in mind, I'm excited to dive into the next chapter, where we'll explore even more strategies for enhancing customer relationships and loyalty. Stay tuned because the best is yet to come.

4

CONTENT AS CURRENCY

Content is a big deal in today's business world. So, what exactly is content? Content is the stuff we put out there to tell our story, connect with our customers, and showcase what we're all about. It could be anything from blog posts and videos to social media updates and podcasts—anything that gets our message across.

Content is essential in today's digital age. It's how we grab people's attention, build relationships, and, ultimately, drive our business forward.

That's where the concept of content as currency comes in. Like money, content has value—we use it to buy our customers' attention and loyalty. And the more valuable our content, the more likely we are to attract and retain customers.

In this chapter, we'll dive deep into the world of content. We'll talk about the different types of content, how to create content that stands out, and the best ways to get our content in front of the right people.

UNDERSTANDING THE VALUE OF CONTENT

Let's talk about the nitty-gritty of content—trust me, it's more than just pretty words on a page.

First, I want to discuss how content helps us reel in those customers. In today's digital world, people are bombarded with information left, right, and center. If we want to stand out from the crowd, we need content that grabs their attention and makes them sit up and take notice.

However, it's not just about getting people in the door—it's about keeping them coming back for more. That's where high-quality, relevant content comes into play. If we're serving up helpful, informative, or entertaining content, people are more likely to stick around and engage with our brand.

Content isn't just a one-time thing—it's an ongoing investment. Every piece of content we put out there is like a little soldier, working tirelessly to spread the word about our business, build trust with our audience, and, ultimately, drive conversions.

Whether a blog post, social media update, or video tutorial, every piece of content we create is like a little gold nugget, adding value to our business and helping us connect with our customers in meaningful ways. And when it comes to building a successful business in today's world, content is king.

TYPES OF CONTENT

There are many different flavors of content out there. It's like a buffet but for your business.

First, there is written content. Written content includes blog posts, articles, and good old-fashioned emails. Written content is great for getting your message across clearly and concisely, and it's perfect for folks who love to curl up with a good read.

Next, there is visual content. Think eye-catching graphics, stunning photos, and attention-grabbing videos. Visual content is all about catching people's attention and making them stop scrolling—after all, a picture is worth a thousand words, right?

And then, there's interactive content. This is the stuff that gets people involved, whether quizzes, polls, or interactive infographics. Interactive content is all about sparking engagement and getting people to participate in your brand.

Remember, different strokes for different folks. Everyone has their preferences when it comes to content. Some people love to read, some love to watch, and some love to get their hands dirty. If we want to connect with our audience, we need to serve up a smorgasbord of content that caters to all tastes.

That's where the magic happens. By creating diverse and engaging content that speaks to different people in different ways, we can reach more people, make a bigger impact, and, ultimately, grow our business. Whether words, pictures, or something in between, let's get creative and start serving up some seriously tasty content.

CREATING COMPELLING CONTENT

Whipping up some seriously captivating content is like cooking up a storm in the kitchen but with words and images instead of ingredients.

Storytelling is key to creating compelling content. People don't just want to hear about your products or services—they want to hear your story. They want to know who you are, what you stand for, and why you do what you do. When it comes to creating content, don't be afraid to get personal. Share your successes, your failures, and everything in between. Be authentic, be genuine, and above all, be yourself.

Regarding content creation, coming up with fresh ideas day in and day out can be a challenge, but it's all about finding inspiration in the world around you. Keep your eyes and ears open, pay attention to what's happening in your industry, and don't be afraid to put your unique spin on things.

Consistency is key, too. Creating content is like building a relationship—it takes time, effort, and dedication. Set a schedule, stick to it, and before you know it, you'll have a library of content sure to impress.

Last but not least, let's talk about SEO. No matter how amazing your content is, it won't do much good if nobody can find it. That's where SEO comes in. By sprinkling some strategic keywords throughout your content and optimizing your metadata, you can help your content climb the ranks and get noticed by the right people.

Whether you're penning a blog post, shooting a video, or designing an infographic, remember to tell your story, stay true to yourself, and keep those SEO best practices in mind. With a little creativity and a lot of hustle, you'll be churning out compelling content that keeps your audience coming back for more.

Distributing Content Effectively

Let's chat about getting our content out there into the big wide world—because what good is a masterpiece if nobody sees it, right?

First, we've got social media. Social media is like a bustling marketplace where people come to hang out, catch up with friends, and discover new things. Therefore, it's the perfect place to share your content and get it in front of a whole bunch of eyeballs. Whether a snappy tweet, a stunning Instagram post, or a thought-provoking LinkedIn article, social media is where the magic happens.

Then, there's email marketing. Email might not be as flashy as social media, but it's still a powerhouse when it comes to content distribution. Email provides a direct line to your audience's inbox, which means you can reach them wherever they are, whenever you want. Plus, with the right tools and techniques, you can personalize your emails, segment your audience, and track your results—all of which can help you get the most out of your email marketing efforts.

And let's not forget about blogging. Blogging might seem old-school compared to social media and email, but it's still one of the most effective ways to share your content and attract new followers. Plus, with the right SEO strategy, you can help your blog posts rank higher in search engine results, meaning more people will find your content when searching for answers to their burning questions.

Regarding content distribution, one size doesn't fit all. Every audience is different, so you must tailor your approach to fit their preferences and behavior. Do your research, experiment with different channels, and see what works best for you.

And don't forget about content scheduling and promotion tools. These handy little helpers can save you time, streamline your workflow, and help you get the most out of your content. Whether scheduling posts in advance, tracking your analytics, or running targeted ads, these tools can help you take your content distribution game to the next level.

Whether sharing your content on social media, sending it out via email, or publishing it on your blog, remember to choose the right channels, personalize your approach, and make the most of those handy tools. With a little strategy and a lot of hustle, you'll be distributing your content like a pro in no time.

ANALYZING CONTENT PERFORMANCE

Once we create our content, how can we tell if it is hitting the mark or not?

First, we have to look at the numbers. You know, things like engagement rates and conversion rates. Engagement rates tell us how many people are interacting with our content—likes, comments, shares, that kind of stuff. Conversion rates tell us how many of those interactions are turning into actions—things like signing up for our email list, downloading a freebie, or making a purchase. These numbers help us determine if our content resonates with our audience and drives the desired results.

However, it's not just about the numbers. We also must pay attention to what our audience is saying. Are they leaving comments on our blog posts? Sending us messages on social media? Asking questions in our emails? These interactions can give us valuable insights into what our audience likes, dislikes, and wants more of. Therefore, listening to their feedback and using it to inform our content strategy is important.

And let's not forget about analytics tools. These nifty little gadgets can help us track our content performance, analyze our audience's behavior, and identify trends over time. Whether Google Analytics, social media insights, or email marketing reports, these tools can give us all the data we need to make informed decisions about our content strategy.

By keeping an eye on the numbers, listening to our audience, and using analytics tools to track our performance, we can make sure our content is hitting the mark and driving the results we want. And if it's not, then it's time to roll up our sleeves, make some tweaks, and try again. After all, that's how we learn and grow as content creators.

Monetizing Content

Now, let's talk about making some cash from all that content we've been creating. Yeah, you heard me right—money!

One way to do it is through affiliate marketing. It's like when we partner up with other businesses and promote their products or services. If someone clicks on our affiliate link and makes a purchase, we get a little kickback. It's a win-win—we make some money, and our audience can access products or services they might find useful.

Another option is sponsored content. This is when companies pay us to create content that features their brand or products. It's kind of like product placement in movies or TV shows. We've got to be careful with this one, though. We don't want to come off as too salesy or lose the trust of our audience. So, it's important to only work with brands that align with our values and provide real value to our audience.

Then, there are premium subscriptions. This is when we offer exclusive content or perks to subscribers who pay a monthly or yearly fee. It's a great way to reward our most loyal fans and generate some steady revenue. Plus, it helps us build a sense of community and connection with our audience.

I'm not saying we should slap ads all over our website or start shoving sponsored content down our audience's throats. That's a surefire way to turn people off and lose their trust. We have to strike a balance between making money and keeping our audience happy. After all, they're the ones who keep coming back for more, so it's important to treat them right.

PROTECTING INTELLECTUAL PROPERTY

Once we create content, keeping it safe and sound is important. You know, making sure nobody's out there stealing our brilliant ideas or using our hard work without permission.

One way to protect our content is by using copyright and trademark protection. Think of copyright as a shield that guards our written content, images, videos, and other creative works. It's automatic—you create something and automatically own the rights to it. However, it's a good idea to slap a little copyright notice on our stuff to let people know we mean business.

Then, there are trademarks. These bad boys protect our brand names, logos, and slogans. They set us apart from the competition and make our business recognizable. We want to make sure nobody's out there trying to pass off their stuff as ours.

There are other strategies we can use to protect our content. One thing we can do is use watermarks on our images and videos. It's like stamping our logo on everything we create—making it harder for people to steal and claim our stuff as their own.

We can also keep an eye out for any shady characters trying to rip us off. That means doing regular searches to see if anyone's using our content without permission. And if we catch someone red-handed, we must be ready to act. That might mean sending a cease-and-desist letter or even taking them to court if things get nasty.

Of course, having a little legal muscle on our side never hurts. That's where legal resources come in handy. Whether hiring a lawyer to help us navigate the legal waters or just brushing up on our rights as content creators, having a little legal know-how can go a long way.

CONCLUSION

As we wrap up this chapter, let's take a quick look at what we've covered.

We started by diving into the world of content—what it is, why it matters, and how it's become the currency of modern business. From blog posts to videos to social media updates, content is what helps us connect with our audience and keep them coming back for more.

We then explored different types of content and how to create compelling stuff that grabs attention and keeps people engaged. Whether a witty blog post or a stunning Instagram photo, the key is to create content that speaks to our audience and adds value to their lives.

Next, we talked about distribution—how to get our content out there and in front of the right people. From social media to email marketing to good old-fashioned blogging, there are plenty of ways to get our message out there and make sure it gets seen.

We also touched on the importance of analyzing our content's performance. By keeping an eye on things like engagement rates and conversion rates, we can see what's working and what's not and adjust accordingly.

Then, we explored the world of monetization—how to turn our content into cold, hard cash. Whether through affiliate marketing, sponsored content, or premium subscriptions, there are plenty of ways to monetize our content and turn our passion into profit.

Finally, we talked about protecting our intellectual property—making sure nobody's out there stealing our stuff and passing it off as their own. From copyrights to trademarks to watermarks, plenty of tools are at our disposal to keep our content safe and sound.

There you have it—content as currency. With the right strategies and a little bit of know-how, we can turn our content into an asset for our business and keep our audience coming back for more. With that, let's prepare for the next chapter, where we'll dive into even more business growth and success strategies.

5

EXTENDING ENGAGEMENT
TO FULFILLMENT

As a business owner, I've realized that ensuring customer satisfaction doesn't end with making a sale. It extends to every step of the journey, including the crucial phase of fulfillment. In this chapter, we'll explore why extending engagement to fulfillment is vital for the success of any business. We'll discuss various strategies aimed at keeping customers engaged and satisfied throughout the fulfillment process. By the end of this chapter, you'll understand how to turn fulfillment into an opportunity to strengthen customer relationships and drive long-term loyalty.

Throughout my years in business, I've learned the journey doesn't stop once a customer clicks "buy." It's essential to recognize that the fulfillment process significantly shapes the overall customer experience. It's the moment when promises are fulfilled, expectations are met, and impressions are made. Therefore, this chapter will focus on strategies to leverage this critical phase to its fullest potential.

In the upcoming sections, we'll delve into various aspects of extending engagement to fulfillment. We'll cover everything from aligning fulfillment with customer expectations to enhancing communication and resolving challenges. By understanding the importance of this phase and implementing the right strategies, we can turn fulfillment into a powerful tool for fostering customer loyalty and satisfaction. Let's dive in and explore how we can make every step of the customer journey count.

UNDERSTANDING FULFILLMENT IN THE CUSTOMER JOURNEY

Fulfillment is more than just shipping out orders. It's a crucial part of the overall customer experience, significantly shaping perceptions and fostering loyalty. When a customer places an order, they're not just buying a product but investing their trust in your brand to deliver on their expectations.

Seamless fulfillment processes are essential for meeting these expectations. Customers expect their orders to be processed efficiently, shipped promptly, and delivered accurately. Any hiccups along the way can lead to frustration and dissatisfaction, potentially tarnishing the relationship with the customer.

Moreover, fulfillment doesn't end when the package arrives at the customer's doorstep. It extends to the entire post-purchase experience, including unboxing, product quality, and customer support. How well you handle these aspects can significantly impact long-term customer satisfaction and loyalty.

In essence, understanding the role of fulfillment in the customer journey is about recognizing its significance beyond the transactional aspect. It's about delivering on promises, exceeding expectations, and ultimately, building trust and loyalty that extend far beyond a single purchase.

ALIGNING FULFILLMENT WITH CUSTOMER EXPECTATIONS

Understanding and meeting customer expectations in the fulfillment process is crucial for building trust and satisfaction. Customers have specific expectations regarding delivery times, packaging, and overall experience when they place an order. Failing to meet these expectations can lead to disappointment and erode their trust in your brand.

I've implemented various strategies to align fulfillment processes with customer preferences and needs. One key approach is offering multiple shipping options to cater to customer preferences. Some prioritize speed, while others prefer lower costs or eco-friendly packaging. By providing choices, we empower customers to select the option that best suits their needs.

Additionally, leveraging data and feedback has continuously improved our fulfillment experiences. We track metrics like delivery times, order accuracy, and customer satisfaction scores to identify areas for improvement. Whether through surveys or direct communication, customer feedback also provides valuable insights into their preferences and pain points. By listening to our customers and adapting our processes accordingly, we can ensure our fulfillment efforts consistently meet or exceed their expectations.

Ultimately, aligning fulfillment with customer expectations is about putting the customer at the center of every decision. By understanding their needs, preferences, and feedback, we can tailor our fulfillment processes to deliver a seamless and satisfying experience that keeps them coming back.

ENHANCING COMMUNICATION DURING FULFILLMENT

In my experience running a business, I've learned that proactive communication during the fulfillment process is essential for keeping customers informed and satisfied. When customers place an order, they appreciate being kept in the loop about its status and any relevant updates. Failure to communicate effectively can lead to uncertainty and frustration, ultimately impacting their perception of our brand.

To address this, we've implemented strategies to provide timely updates and notifications to our customers throughout the fulfillment journey. This includes sending confirmation emails immediately after an order is placed, detailing the expected delivery timeframe, and providing tracking information as soon as it becomes available. We ensure transparency and build trust in our processes by keeping customers informed every step of the way.

Technology and automation have been invaluable tools in streamlining communication during fulfillment. We use automated systems to send out notifications at key milestones, such as when an order is shipped or out for delivery. This saves time and ensures consistency in our messaging. Additionally, we leverage technology to provide self-service options for customers to track their orders or modify delivery preferences, further enhancing their experience.

By prioritizing proactive communication and leveraging technology, we aim to make the fulfillment process as smooth and transparent as possible for our customers. This helps manage their expectations and reinforces our commitment to delivering exceptional service at every touchpoint.

PERSONALIZING THE FULFILLMENT EXPERIENCE

In my business journey, I've come to understand the importance of tailoring the fulfillment experience to each customer's unique preferences. It's not just about getting the product to their doorstep; it's about making that entire process feel special and tailored just for them.

One strategy we've adopted is personalizing packaging and delivery options. For instance, if we know a customer prefers eco-friendly packaging, we make sure to use recyclable materials and include a note thanking them for their commitment to sustainability. Similarly, we offer expedited shipping options for customers who value speed to ensure their orders arrive as quickly as possible.

Post-purchase interactions also play a crucial role in personalizing the fulfillment experience. We send follow-up emails or make courtesy calls to check if everything arrived as expected and if they're satisfied with their purchase. This shows that we care about their experience and provides an opportunity to address their concerns.

Incorporating customization and personal touches is another way we enhance the fulfillment experience. This could be as simple as including a handwritten thank-you note or offering complimentary samples related to their purchase. These small gestures go a long way in making customers feel valued and appreciated.

By personalizing the fulfillment experience, we not only meet customer expectations but also exceed them. It's about creating a connection with our customers and showing them that we understand and care about their individual needs and preferences. Ultimately, this leads to stronger relationships and increased loyalty to our brand.

Resolving Fulfillment Issues
and Challenges

While running my business, I've encountered various fulfillment issues and challenges that can arise, impacting the customer experience. Whether a delayed shipment, a damaged product upon arrival, or a mix-up in the order, these issues can undermine customer satisfaction if not handled promptly and effectively.

One common challenge is shipping delays, which can occur due to logistical issues or unforeseen circumstances like weather disruptions. When faced with such challenges, it's essential to communicate transparently with customers, providing updates on the status of their orders and offering alternative solutions, if possible, such as expedited shipping at no extra cost.

Another issue is receiving damaged or defective products, which can happen despite our best efforts to ensure quality control. In such cases, we prioritize quick resolution by offering refunds, replacements, or store credits, depending on the customer's preference. Additionally, we take steps to investigate the root cause of the problem and implement corrective measures to prevent similar issues in the future.

Sometimes, fulfillment challenges stem from miscommunications or errors in the ordering process. For instance, customers may receive the wrong item or size due to inaccuracies in the order fulfillment system. To address these issues, we have streamlined our internal processes and invested in technology to minimize human error. Additionally, we offer hassle-free returns and exchanges to promptly rectify mistakes and ensure customer satisfaction.

To illustrate the effectiveness of these strategies, let me share a recent case study. After receiving a damaged product, a customer contacted us, expressing disappointment and frustration. We immediately apologized for the inconvenience and offered a replacement at no extra cost and a discount on their next purchase as a gesture of goodwill. Our swift response and generous resolution impressed the customer, leading to a positive outcome and continued loyalty to our brand.

In summary, by proactively identifying and addressing fulfillment issues, we can uphold our commitment to providing exceptional customer service and ensure a seamless experience from purchase to delivery.

MEASURING FULFILLMENT SUCCESS

In my business, ensuring that our fulfillment processes run smoothly is crucial to keeping our customers happy and returning for more. To gauge how well we're doing in this department, we've identified some key metrics to track our fulfillment effectiveness.

One important indicator we look at is our order accuracy rate. This tells us how often we get orders right the first time without any mistakes or mix-ups. We track this closely because accuracy is essential for customer satisfaction. If orders are consistently incorrect, it can lead to frustration and loss of trust.

Another metric we pay close attention to is our fulfillment speed. We want to ensure we get orders out the door and into customers' hands as quickly as possible. Speedy fulfillment not only delights customers but also reduces the risk of delays and potential issues along the way.

We also measure our on-time delivery rate. This tells us how often we meet our promised delivery dates. Timely delivery is crucial for customer satisfaction, especially for time-sensitive orders. If we're consistently missing delivery deadlines, it's a sign that we need to reassess our logistics and shipping processes.

In addition to these KPIs, we gather customer feedback about their fulfillment experience. This can come through surveys, reviews, or direct communication. By listening to what our customers have to say, we gain valuable insights into what we're doing well and where we can improve.

To analyze all this data, we rely on analytics tools that help us track our fulfillment metrics over time. These tools allow us to spot trends, identify areas for improvement, and make data-driven decisions to optimize our fulfillment processes.

By closely monitoring these KPIs and leveraging customer feedback and analytics, we can continuously measure our fulfillment success and adjust as needed to ensure we're delivering the best possible experience to our customers.

BUILDING LOYALTY THROUGH EXCEPTIONAL FULFILLMENT

Exceptional fulfillment isn't just about getting orders out the door—it's about creating moments customers remember and cherish. I've seen firsthand how these experiences can turn first-time buyers into loyal advocates for our brand.

We aim to exceed customer expectations by going above and beyond in every aspect of fulfillment. From the moment an order is placed to the minute it arrives at their doorstep, we strive to make the entire process seamless and delightful. This means paying attention to the little details, like carefully packaging items, providing personalized notes or surprises, and ensuring timely delivery.

However, exceptional fulfillment goes beyond just getting the basics right. It's about finding unique ways to surprise and delight our customers. For example, we might include a handwritten thank-you note with every order or offer free expedited shipping as a surprise upgrade. These small gestures may seem simple, but they can leave a lasting impression and make customers feel valued and appreciated.

In addition to providing exceptional fulfillment experiences, we've also implemented loyalty programs and incentives to reward our most loyal customers. These programs encourage repeat business and incentivize customers to refer their friends and family to our brand. By offering rewards like discounts, exclusive access to products or events, or even cashback incentives, we can show our appreciation for their continued support and help foster a sense of community around our brand.

Ultimately, by delivering exceptional fulfillment experiences and rewarding customer loyalty, we can build strong relationships with our customers that extend far beyond individual transactions. And in today's competitive marketplace, cultivating these relationships is key to our long-term success.

Conclusion

As we wrap up this chapter, it's crucial to reflect on the essential aspects we've covered regarding extending engagement to fulfillment. We've journeyed through the significance of exceeding customer expectations during the fulfillment process. From understanding the role of fulfillment in the customer journey to aligning our processes with their preferences, we've explored how every step impacts long-term satisfaction and loyalty.

Throughout our discussion, one key theme emerged: Exceptional fulfillment isn't just about getting orders out the door; it's about creating memorable experiences that leave a lasting impression on our customers. We've seen how personalized communication, proactive problem-solving, and continuous improvement are integral to achieving this goal.

Moreover, we've emphasized the importance of measuring fulfillment success through key performance indicators and gathering feedback to identify areas for improvement. By leveraging data and analytics, we can continually refine our processes and better serve our customers.

As we look ahead, it's clear that extending engagement to fulfillment is just one piece of the puzzle. In the chapters to come, we'll explore additional strategies for enhancing customer relationships and loyalty beyond the fulfillment experience. From nurturing ongoing communication to building brand advocacy, we'll continue to uncover insights and practical approaches for cultivating meaningful connections with our customers.

In summary, we're laying the foundation for long-term satisfaction and loyalty by prioritizing exceptional fulfillment and extending engagement throughout the entire customer journey. And with each interaction, we can deepen our relationships and create value that extends far beyond individual transactions.

6

CAPITALIZING ON AUTO PAYMENTS

In today's fast-paced business landscape, where convenience and efficiency are paramount, auto payments have emerged as a cornerstone of modern commerce. As a business owner, I've witnessed firsthand the transformative power of auto payments in streamlining transactions and fostering customer loyalty. In this chapter, we'll explore how businesses can capitalize on auto payments to optimize their operations and enhance the overall customer experience.

Auto payments, also known as automatic payments or recurring payments, have become ubiquitous in modern business practices. They allow customers to set up automatic withdrawals from their accounts to pay for goods or services on a regular basis, eliminating the need for manual transactions. This simplifies the payment process for customers and ensures a steady and predictable revenue stream for businesses.

The primary focus of this chapter is to delve into the various ways businesses can leverage auto payments to their advantage. From improving cash flow management to increasing customer retention, auto payments offer a multitude of benefits for businesses of all sizes. Throughout the chapter, we'll discuss strategies for optimizing auto payment systems, analyzing performance metrics, and mitigating potential risks.

By the end of this chapter, you'll have a comprehensive understanding of how auto payments can be a game-changer for your business and how to harness their full potential to drive growth and success.

UNDERSTANDING AUTO PAYMENTS

Understanding auto payments is crucial for any business looking to streamline its operations and improve customer satisfaction. Essentially, auto payments refer to the automated process of charging customers for goods or services on a recurring basis. It's like setting your bills on autopilot, ensuring they're paid without the hassle of manual transactions each time.

Why are auto payments so significant? Imagine this: Your customers sign up for your service or purchase a subscription, and instead of having to remember to pay every month, the amount is automatically deducted from their account. This seamless process saves them time and effort and reduces the risk of missed payments, which can lead to frustration and potential churn.

However, it's not just about convenience for the customer; auto payments also substantially impact your business's bottom line. By implementing auto payment systems, you can ensure a steady and predictable stream of revenue, which is essential for budgeting and planning. Plus, with automatic payments processed, you can improve cash flow management and reduce the administrative burden of manual invoicing and collection.

Auto payments are the backbone of modern business transactions, providing customers and businesses with unparalleled convenience and efficiency. By understanding their significance and optimizing your auto payment processes, you can enhance the customer experience and drive sustainable growth for your business.

IMPLEMENTING AUTO PAYMENT SYSTEMS

Implementing auto payment systems in my business was a game-changer. It wasn't just about making transactions smoother for our customers but also about streamlining our internal processes and ensuring financial stability.

When it comes to setting up auto payment systems, there are a few key strategies that I found to be effective. First and foremost, it's crucial to choose the right payment platform and provider. I researched different options, considering factors like ease of integration, transaction fees, and customer support. Finding a provider that aligns with your business needs and values is essential for a seamless implementation process.

Once we selected our payment platform, the next step was ensuring security and compliance. With auto payments, sensitive financial information is being exchanged, so it's paramount to prioritize data security and adhere to industry regulations. We took proactive measures to implement robust security protocols and regularly update our systems to avoid potential threats.

Additionally, we didn't overlook the importance of educating our customers about auto payments. We communicated clearly about the process, outlining the benefits and addressing any concerns they might have had. Transparency and trust are crucial when it comes to financial transactions, so keeping our customers informed every step of the way is a top priority.

Implementing auto payment systems required careful planning and execution, but the payoff was well worth it. It enhanced the customer experience by providing greater convenience, streamlined our operations, and improved our financial stability. By selecting the right payment provider, prioritizing security and compliance, and keeping our customers informed, we successfully implemented auto payment systems and reap the benefits for our business.

Optimizing Auto Payment Experiences

Optimizing our auto payment experience has been a key focus for my business. It's not just about automating transactions; it's about making sure our customers have a seamless and hassle-free experience every step of the way.

One of the most critical aspects of optimizing auto payments is simplifying the setup and management process. We realized early on that if the setup process was too complicated or time-consuming, customers would be less likely to enroll in auto payments. So, we streamlined the process as much as possible, minimizing the number of steps required and providing clear instructions along the way.

We also made sure to incorporate personalized touches to enhance the auto payment experience. Instead of treating auto payments as a one-size-fits-all solution, we tailored our approach to each individual customer. This meant offering flexible payment options, such as choosing the best billing cycle for them and providing personalized support whenever needed.

In addition to simplifying the setup process and adding personalized touches, we continuously monitor and optimize our auto payment systems to ensure they're meeting the needs of our customers. This involves regularly gathering feedback, analyzing data, and adjusting as necessary to improve the overall experience.

By prioritizing simplicity, personalization, and ongoing optimization, we've created an auto payment experience that saves our customers time and effort and strengthens their trust and loyalty to our business. As we continue to refine and improve our processes, we're confident that our auto payment system will remain a valuable asset for our customers and our business.

LEVERAGING AUTO PAYMENTS FOR BUSINESS GROWTH

Leveraging auto payments for our business growth has been a game-changer. It's not just about making transactions easier for our customers; it's about using this tool strategically to strengthen our relationships with them and keep them coming back.

We've leveraged auto payments for business growth by focusing on increasing customer retention and loyalty. By offering auto payment options, we make it more convenient for our customers to continue doing business with us. This convenience encourages them to stick around longer, ultimately boosting our retention rates. Plus, when customers set their payments to auto, they're less likely to forget or delay payments, reducing the risk of churn.

Another strategy we've employed is to incentivize customers to enroll in auto payments. We offer exclusive discounts or rewards to customers who opt for this payment method, giving them an extra incentive to choose auto payments over manual ones. Not only does this help increase enrollment rates, but it also strengthens our relationships with our most loyal customers.

To illustrate the effectiveness of our auto payment strategies, we can look at some case studies. For example, we had a customer who was initially hesitant to enroll in auto payments due to security concerns. However, after we assured them of our robust security measures and offered them a discount for enrolling, they decided to give it a try. Not only did they enjoy the convenience of auto payments, but they also became one of our most loyal customers, consistently renewing their subscriptions year after year.

By strategically leveraging auto payments to increase customer retention and loyalty, we've fueled our business growth and created a more stable and sustainable revenue stream. As we continue to refine our auto payment strategies based on customer feedback and market insights, we're confident that this tool will remain a powerful driver of our success.

ANALYZING AUTO PAYMENT PERFORMANCE

Analyzing the performance of our auto payment system has been instrumental in fine-tuning our approach and ensuring it aligns with our business objectives. By identifying key metrics and gathering customer feedback, we can gain valuable insights into how well our auto payment system is performing and where there may be room for improvement.

One crucial metric we track is the enrollment rate for auto payments. This tells us how many customers are opting to use this payment method, indicating its popularity and effectiveness. Additionally, we monitor the retention rate of customers who use auto payments compared to those who don't. This helps us understand the impact of auto payments on customer loyalty and long-term engagement.

Gathering feedback from our customers is equally important. We regularly solicit input through surveys, interviews, and direct interactions to understand their experiences with our auto payment system. This feedback allows us to identify pain points, address any issues promptly, and adjust to improve the overall user experience.

To analyze auto payment performance effectively, we utilize analytics tools that provide us with valuable data and insights. These tools allow us to track key metrics in real time, identify trends and patterns, and make data-driven decisions about our auto payment strategy. For example, we can see which payment methods are most popular among our customers, which subscription plans have the highest auto payment enrollment rates, and how auto payments impact our revenue and cash flow.

By regularly analyzing auto payment performance and making informed adjustments based on our findings, we can ensure that our system remains effective in driving customer engagement, loyalty, and business growth.

Mitigating Risks Associated with Auto Payments

Mitigating risks tied to auto payments is vital to ensuring smooth and secure transactions for my customers and my business. Identifying potential risks and challenges associated with auto payments is the first step toward developing effective strategies to address them.

One common risk is security breaches, where sensitive customer information may be compromised. To mitigate this risk, I implement robust security measures such as encryption protocols and regular security audits to safeguard customer data. Additionally, I stay informed about the latest cybersecurity threats and continuously update our security protocols to stay ahead of potential risks.

Another challenge is fraud, where unauthorized transactions may occur. To combat this, I implement strict authentication procedures, such as requiring multi-factor authentication for auto-payment setups and regularly monitoring transactions for any suspicious activity. By staying vigilant and promptly addressing any signs of fraud, I can protect my customers and business from potential financial losses.

Payment failures are another risk associated with auto payments, which can lead to customer dissatisfaction and loss of revenue. To mitigate this risk, I implement redundant payment processing systems and regularly monitor transaction logs to promptly identify and address any issues. Additionally, I provide clear communication channels for customers to report payment failures and offer prompt assistance to resolve any issues they encounter.

Managing auto payment-related disputes and issues is essential for maintaining customer trust and satisfaction. I ensure that my customer service team is well-trained in handling payment-related inquiries and disputes, providing timely and empathetic assistance to customers who encounter issues with their auto payments. By addressing customer concerns promptly and effectively, I can minimize the impact of disputes on customer satisfaction and retention.

Overall, by identifying potential risks associated with auto payments and implementing effective strategies to mitigate them, I can ensure a secure and reliable payment experience for my customers while safeguarding the financial interests of my business.

Expanding Auto Payment Offerings

Expanding our auto payment offerings is crucial for keeping up with our customers' evolving needs and preferences. As our business grows, we must provide various convenient payment options catering to different customer preferences and lifestyles.

Introducing new auto payment options and features requires careful planning and consideration. We start by analyzing customer feedback and market trends to identify the most in-demand payment methods and features. For example, if our customers express interest in recurring billing options or alternative payment methods like digital wallets, we prioritize implementing these features into our auto payment offerings.

Scaling our auto payment capabilities as our business expands is also a key consideration. We ensure that our payment processing systems can handle increased transaction volumes without sacrificing performance or security. This may involve upgrading our infrastructure, investing in more advanced payment processing technologies, or partnering with reliable payment service providers to accommodate our growing customer base.

Additionally, we keep abreast of regulatory requirements and industry standards to ensure compliance as we expand our auto payment offerings. Staying compliant with relevant regulations protects our customers' data and helps us build trust and credibility in the marketplace.

By continuously expanding and refining our auto payment offerings, we can better meet the diverse needs of our customers while driving growth and success for our business.

Conclusion

In wrapping up this chapter, let's take a moment to recap what we've covered regarding capitalizing on auto payments in our business operations.

We began by understanding the significance of auto payments in modern business transactions. These automated payment processes enhance convenience for our customers and play a crucial role in improving our revenue streams and cash flow management.

We then delved into the implementation of auto-payment systems, exploring strategies for selecting the right platforms and ensuring security and compliance. By carefully choosing our payment providers and prioritizing data security, we can offer our customers seamless and trustworthy auto payment experiences.

Optimizing the auto payment experience emerged as another key focus. We discussed the importance of simplifying setup processes and incorporating personalization to enhance customer satisfaction. We can foster stronger relationships and increase loyalty by making it easy and enjoyable for customers to manage their auto payments.

Analyzing auto payment performance was also highlighted, emphasizing the need to track key metrics and gather feedback to make informed decisions. By leveraging analytics tools, we can identify areas for improvement and refine our auto payment strategies to better meet customer needs.

Lastly, we explored strategies for mitigating risks associated with auto payments, ensuring that our systems are secure and resilient against fraud and payment failures. By implementing best practices for dispute resolution and risk management, we can maintain the trust and confidence of our customers.

Capitalizing on auto payments is essential for driving business success. By offering convenient, secure, and personalized payment experiences, we can enhance customer satisfaction, increase retention, and ultimately achieve our business goals.

Our journey continues with upcoming chapters focusing on additional strategies for optimizing customer transactions. Stay tuned as we explore new avenues for growth and innovation in our business operations.

7

CASE STUDY: EVERGOOD ADVENTURE WINES

Welcome to the captivating world of Evergood Adventure Wines, where every sip tells a story of exploration, discovery, and celebration. As the founder and CEO of Evergood Adventure Wines, I am thrilled to share our winery journey with you through this case study.

Our story began with a passion for both wine and adventure. Inspired by the beauty of the great outdoors and the joy of sharing memorable moments with loved ones, I set out to create a wine brand that embodies the spirit of adventure. Evergood Adventure Wines was born out of this vision, with a mission to craft exceptional wines that capture the essence of our natural landscapes and inspire moments of connection and adventure.

In this case study, we'll delve into the heart of Evergood Adventure Wines, exploring the strategies, challenges, and triumphs that have shaped our journey. From our humble beginnings to our current standing in the market, we'll uncover the secrets behind our success and the lessons learned along the way.

Throughout this chapter, we'll examine key aspects of our business, including our marketing strategy, product development approach, distribution channels, customer engagement initiatives, and overall impact on the wine industry. By gaining insights into Evergood Adventure Wines, I hope to provide valuable knowledge and inspiration to fellow entrepreneurs and wine enthusiasts.

So, grab a glass of your favorite Evergood Adventure Wine, sit back, and join me as we embark on this exciting exploration of our winery's story. Cheers to the adventure ahead!

BACKGROUND OF EVERGOOD ADVENTURE WINES

Evergood Adventure Wines isn't just a winery; it's a testament to my passion for crafting exceptional wines and sharing unforgettable experiences. Our journey began with a simple yet powerful vision: to create wines that capture the essence of adventure and inspire people to savor life's most memorable moments.

As the founder of Evergood Adventure Wines, I embarked on this venture with a clear mission: to craft wines embodying the spirit of exploration and celebration. Drawing inspiration from my love for adventure and the great outdoors, I set out to create wines that evoke a sense of wonder and excitement with every sip.

I was met with a diverse and dynamic landscape when I first entered the wine industry. From established vineyards to emerging boutique wineries, the industry offered challenges and opportunities for newcomers like Evergood Adventure Wines. Despite the competition, I saw an opportunity to carve out a unique niche by blending my passion for adventure with the art of winemaking.

Of course, building Evergood Adventure Wines from the ground up wasn't without its hurdles. Like any entrepreneurial endeavor, we faced our fair share of challenges along the way. From sourcing quality grapes to establishing distribution channels, every step of the journey presented its own set of obstacles to overcome.

However, with determination and a commitment to our vision, we embraced these challenges as opportunities for growth. We approached each setback as a chance to learn and innovate, refining our approach and staying true to our mission every step of the way.

Today, Evergood Adventure Wines stands as a testament to the power of passion, perseverance, and the pursuit of adventure. Our wines continue to delight enthusiasts and adventurers alike, inviting them to raise a glass to the endless possibilities that await.

MARKETING STRATEGY

Crafting a compelling marketing strategy has been pivotal in the success of Evergood Adventure Wines. From the outset, we knew that effectively positioning our brand and connecting with our target audience would be essential for building awareness and driving sales.

Our brand positioning centers around the idea of adventure and exploration. We've honed in on consumers who share our love for the outdoors, travel, and experiencing life to the fullest. By aligning our brand with these values, we've resonated with a niche audience seeking more than just a great bottle of wine—they're looking for an experience.

Regarding marketing channels, we've embraced a multi-faceted approach to reach our audience where they are. Social media has played a significant role in our strategy, allowing us to showcase the adventurous spirit behind our wines and engage with our community directly. Platforms like Instagram and Facebook have provided a platform for sharing stunning imagery, behind-the-scenes glimpses, and stories that bring our brand to life.

Additionally, we've leveraged partnerships and collaborations with outdoor influencers, adventure bloggers, and travel enthusiasts to expand our reach and tap into new audiences. By aligning ourselves with like-minded individuals and organizations, we've amplified our message and extended our reach far beyond traditional marketing channels.

One of our key unique selling propositions is our commitment to quality and sustainability. We prioritize environmentally friendly practices and ethically sourced ingredients from the vineyard to the bottle. This commitment to sustainability sets us apart in a crowded market and resonates with consumers who value authenticity and responsibility.

Furthermore, our competitive advantage lies in our ability to offer wines that taste great and evoke a sense of adventure and discovery. Whether through our unique flavor profiles, innovative packaging, or immersive branding, we strive to offer a one-of-a-kind experience that keeps customers coming back for more.

PRODUCT DEVELOPMENT

In developing our product line at Evergood Adventure Wines, we've strived to offer a diverse range of offerings that cater to various tastes and preferences. From crisp whites perfect for warm summer days to robust reds that pair perfectly with cozy nights by the fire, our goal has been to provide something for every palate and occasion.

In addition to focusing on flavor profiles and varietals, we've also strongly emphasized innovation in packaging and labeling. We recognize that packaging plays a crucial role in shaping consumers' perceptions and influencing purchasing decisions. As such, we've invested in eye-catching labels and environmentally friendly packaging options that stand out on the shelf and reflect our brand's commitment to sustainability.

Customer feedback has been invaluable in guiding our product development efforts. We've made it a priority to actively listen to our customers, whether through direct communication, surveys, or social media interactions. By understanding their preferences, tastes, and desires, we've refined our offerings and introduced new products that better meet their needs.

For example, based on customer feedback, we've expanded our range to include more low-alcohol options for those seeking lighter, more sessionable wines. Additionally, we've introduced packaging innovations such as single-serve cans and portable pouches to cater to outdoor enthusiasts and on-the-go consumers.

Ultimately, our approach to product development is rooted in a deep understanding of our customers and a commitment to delivering high-quality, innovative products that enhance their overall experience with our brand. By staying agile, responsive, and customer-focused, we continue pushing the boundaries of what's possible in adventure wines.

DISTRIBUTION AND SALES

When it comes to getting our wines into the hands of consumers, distribution is key. We've forged partnerships with various distribution channels, from local retailers and specialty wine shops to online marketplaces and subscription services. These partnerships have allowed us to reach a broad audience and make our wines accessible to customers wherever they are.

In terms of sales strategies, we've adopted a multi-faceted approach that combines traditional tactics with innovative techniques. We leverage our relationships with retailers to secure prominent shelf placement and run promotions and tastings to drive in-store sales. At the same time, we've invested in digital marketing and e-commerce platforms to capture the growing online market and connect with consumers directly. Expanding into new markets and customer segments has been a key focus for us as we look to grow our business. We've identified emerging trends and consumer preferences and tailored our offerings to appeal to these new demographics. For example, recognizing the rising interest in organic and sustainable products, we've expanded our presence in natural food stores and eco-conscious markets.

Additionally, we've explored opportunities to enter new geographic markets domestically and internationally. By partnering with distributors and retailers in these regions and adapting our marketing and sales strategies to local preferences, we've successfully introduced our wines to new audiences.

A commitment to accessibility, innovation, and strategic growth guides our distribution and sales efforts. By continuously evaluating market trends, seeking out new opportunities, and refining our approach, we're confident in our ability to continue expanding our reach and delighting customers with our wines.

CUSTOMER ENGAGEMENT AND LOYALTY

For us at Evergood Adventure Wines, fostering strong relationships with our customers isn't just a business strategy—it's at the heart of everything we do. We've developed a range of strategies to engage with our customers and build lasting connections.

One of our primary focuses is on providing exceptional customer service at every touchpoint. Whether it's through our website, social media channels, or in-person interactions, we strive to make every interaction with our customers memorable and positive. From promptly responding to inquiries and addressing concerns to exceeding expectations, we're committed to delivering top-notch service.

In addition to excellent service, we've implemented a loyalty program to reward our most dedicated customers. Through this program, customers earn points for every purchase they make, which can be redeemed for discounts, exclusive offers, and other perks. Not only does this incentivize repeat purchases, but it also reinforces our appreciation for our loyal patrons.

Moreover, we understand the importance of listening to and valuing customers' feedback. We actively solicit feedback through surveys, reviews, and social media channels and carefully consider each comment and suggestion. When customers express concerns or issues, we respond promptly and transparently, proactively addressing their needs and ensuring their satisfaction.

By prioritizing customer engagement and loyalty, we've cultivated a community of passionate wine enthusiasts who enjoy our products and feel a sense of connection to our brand. This ongoing dialogue with our customers strengthens our relationships and helps us continuously improve and evolve to better meet their needs and preferences.

BUSINESS GROWTH AND SUCCESS

As we reflect on the journey of Evergood Adventure Wines, I'm proud to say that we've achieved significant milestones that have propelled our business forward. From our humble beginnings to where we stand today, it's been an incredible ride filled with both challenges and triumphs.

One of our most notable milestones is the expansion of our product line. Over the years, we've introduced new and innovative wine offerings that have resonated with our customers and helped us diversify our portfolio. Each new product launch has allowed us to reach new audiences and expand our market presence, from classic varietals to unique blends. In terms of financial performance, we've seen steady revenue growth year over year. Our commitment to quality, innovation, and customer satisfaction has translated into strong sales and a loyal customer base. By staying true to our values and continuously striving for excellence, we've achieved sustainable financial success while reinvesting in our business for future growth.

Along the way, we've encountered our fair share of challenges. Whether navigating regulatory hurdles, adapting to changing consumer preferences, or overcoming supply chain disruptions, each challenge has presented an opportunity for us to learn and grow. Through perseverance, creativity, and a willingness to embrace change, we've been able to overcome these obstacles and emerge stronger than ever.

We look to the future filled with optimism and excitement. We remain committed to pushing the boundaries of what's possible in the wine industry, exploring new markets, and innovating our products and services to meet the evolving needs of our customers. With a dedicated team, a loyal customer base, and a passion for excellence, the sky's the limit for Evergood Adventure Wines.

IMPACT OF EVERGOOD ADVENTURE WINES

Reflecting on the impact of Evergood Adventure Wines goes beyond just the bottom line. While our business is centered around crafting exceptional wines, our commitment extends far beyond the vineyards and into the communities we serve.

One aspect of our impact that we're particularly proud of is our dedication to social and environmental initiatives. From sustainable farming practices to reducing our carbon footprint, we're constantly striving to minimize our impact on the planet. By prioritizing eco-friendly practices throughout our production process, we're doing our part to preserve the environment for future generations.

In addition to our environmental efforts, we're also deeply invested in giving back to the communities that have supported us along the way. Whether it's through charitable donations, volunteering, or hosting community events, we're always looking for ways to make a positive difference locally. By supporting local businesses, organizations, and initiatives, we're helping to foster vibrant and thriving communities.

Our commitment to excellence has also been recognized on a broader scale, with Evergood Adventure Wines receiving numerous awards and accolades for our outstanding products and contributions to the industry. These honors serve as a testament to our team's hard work and dedication, and they inspire us to continue pushing the boundaries of what's possible in the world of wine.

Overall, the impact of Evergood Adventure Wines extends far beyond the bottles we produce. Through our social and environmental initiatives, contributions to local communities, and recognition within the industry, we're proud to be making a positive difference in the world, one sip at a time.

CONCLUSION

As I reflect on the journey of Evergood Adventure Wines, I'm reminded of the key insights and lessons learned along the way. Our story has been one of passion, perseverance, and continuous growth, and there are several valuable takeaways that I believe can benefit businesses of all sizes.

First, our commitment to quality and innovation has been a driving force behind our success. By staying true to our founding mission and constantly pushing the boundaries of what's possible in the world of wine, we've been able to differentiate ourselves in a competitive market and attract a loyal customer base.

Another key lesson we've learned is the importance of customer engagement and loyalty. By prioritizing personalized experiences, implementing loyalty programs, and actively seeking feedback from our customers, we've built strong relationships and fostered a sense of community around our brand.

Additionally, our journey has taught us the value of adaptability and resilience. From navigating challenges in the industry to seizing growth opportunities, we've remained flexible and agile in our approach, always willing to evolve and innovate to meet the changing needs of our customers.

As I look to the future, I'm filled with gratitude for the incredible journey that Evergood Adventure Wines has embarked on. I'm incredibly proud of what we've accomplished so far, and I'm excited to continue pushing the boundaries and exploring new opportunities for growth and success.

In closing, I want to express my heartfelt appreciation to everyone who has been a part of Evergood Adventure Wines' journey—from our dedicated team members to our loyal customers and partners. It's been an incredible ride, and I can't wait to see what the future holds for our brand. Cheers to the next chapter!

8

BEST PRACTICES FOR SUSTAINABLE ENGAGEMENT

As I delve into the topic of sustainable engagement, it's important to understand its significance in today's business landscape. Sustainability is a fundamental aspect of how modern businesses operate. When we talk about sustainability, we're not just referring to environmental practices, although that's certainly a big part of it. Sustainability in business encompasses a broader range of factors, including social responsibility, ethical business practices, and long-term viability.

In this chapter, we'll explore why sustainability matters in business practices and how it can be integrated into various aspects of operations. By prioritizing sustainability, businesses can reduce their environmental footprint and build stronger relationships with customers, employees, and communities.

This chapter will discuss different strategies and best practices for incorporating sustainability into business operations. From sustainable product development to supply chain management and stakeholder engagement, there are numerous ways for businesses to embrace sustainability and make a positive impact.

UNDERSTANDING SUSTAINABLE ENGAGEMENT

Understanding sustainable engagement is essential for any business owner looking to operate in a socially and environmentally responsible manner. Sustainable engagement goes beyond just selling products or services—it's about building long-term relationships with customers, employees, and communities while minimizing negative impacts on the planet.

At its core, sustainable engagement involves considering the broader implications of business decisions and actions. It means considering the environmental, social, and economic aspects of operations and striving to make choices that benefit all stakeholders.

For me, grasping the concept of sustainable engagement meant recognizing that my business's success isn't just measured by financial metrics but also by its impact on people and the planet. It's about understanding the interconnectedness of our actions and their consequences.

In practical terms, sustainable engagement can manifest in various ways. It could mean sourcing materials from ethical suppliers, implementing energy-efficient practices, supporting local communities through philanthropic initiatives, or ensuring fair labor practices throughout the supply chain.

By understanding sustainable engagement, I've been able to align my business practices with my values and contribute positively to society and the environment. It's about making choices that not only benefit my bottom line but also create a better world for future generations.

Sustainable engagement is the heartbeat of my business philosophy. It's a guiding principle that shapes how I interact with my customers, employees, and the world around me. Simply put, sustainable engagement fosters relationships and practices that endure while considering their impact on people and the planet.

Sustainable engagement is more than just a set of actions or policies—it's a mindset. It's about recognizing that every decision, big or small, has consequences that ripple outward. It's about taking responsibility for those consequences and striving to make choices that contribute positively to the well-being of others and the environment.

In my business, sustainable engagement means prioritizing transparency, honesty, and integrity in all my interactions. It means listening to my customers and employees, understanding their needs and concerns, and working collaboratively to find solutions that benefit everyone involved.

However, sustainable engagement encompasses not just relationships but environmental stewardship. It means reducing waste, conserving resources, and minimizing my carbon footprint wherever possible. It means looking for innovative ways to operate more sustainably and leaving the world a little better than I found it.

Ultimately, sustainable engagement is about building a business that thrives in harmony with its surroundings. It's about creating a legacy that extends far beyond profits and numbers—a legacy of positive impact and lasting relationships.

Sustainability isn't just a trend—it's the cornerstone of my business ethos. Why? Because I firmly believe that it's the key to building strong, long-lasting relationships with my customers, employees, and the wider community.

When prioritizing sustainability in my business practices, I send a powerful message to my customers. I'm showing them that I care about more than just making a profit—I care about our world and the future we're creating together. And that resonates with people. In today's world, consumers are increasingly conscious of their purchases' environmental and social impact. By aligning myself with their values, I'm not just selling products or services but building trust and loyalty.

However, sustainability isn't just about ticking boxes or meeting quotas. It's about embodying a set of principles that guide every decision I make. These principles include things like transparency, integrity, and accountability. It's about being open and honest with my customers and stakeholders, even when it's difficult. It's about doing the right thing, even when no one is watching. And it's about taking responsibility for my actions and their consequences, both now and in the future.

At its core, sustainable engagement is about building relationships that stand the test of time. Sustainable engagement fosters connections based on mutual respect, trust, and shared values. Consistently applying these principles strengthens my business and contributes to a better, more sustainable world.

Building a Sustainable Brand

Building a sustainable brand isn't just about slapping a green logo on my products—it's about embodying sustainability in everything I do. Every aspect of my business reflects my commitment to sustainability, from how I source materials to how I treat my employees.

One of the first steps in building a sustainable brand is incorporating sustainability into my brand identity and values. This means defining what sustainability means to me and my business and integrating it into my mission statement, vision, and core values. For me, sustainability isn't just about protecting the environment—it's also about promoting social equity and economic prosperity. By clearly articulating my commitment to these principles, I can attract like-minded customers and employees who share my values.

However, words alone aren't enough—I also need to walk the walk. That means communicating my sustainability efforts transparently and authentically to my customers. Whether through my website, social media channels, or product packaging, I highlight the steps I'm taking to reduce my environmental impact, support local communities, and promote ethical business practices. By being honest and transparent about my sustainability initiatives, I build trust with my customers and show them I'm serious about making a difference.

Building a sustainable brand also requires aligning my business practices with my sustainable values. This means making conscious choices about everything from sourcing raw materials to manufacturing processes to distribution methods. For example, I might work with suppliers, prioritizing fair labor practices and environmentally friendly production methods. Or I might invest in renewable energy sources to power my operations. By consistently making choices that reflect my commitment to sustainability, I build a stronger brand and contribute to a more sustainable future for us all.

Sustainable Product Development

When it comes to creating sustainable products, I've learned that every decision counts. From where I source my materials to how I package my products, every step of the process minimizes my environmental footprint and maximizes my positive impact.

First, sustainable product development starts with sustainable sourcing and production methods. Instead of simply going for the cheapest option, I take the time to research suppliers who prioritize ethical labor practices and environmentally friendly production processes. Whether using organic cotton for my clothing line or choosing responsibly sourced wood for my furniture, I make sure that every material I use meets rigorous sustainability standards.

However, sustainability isn't just about the materials but also the design. That's why I'm always looking for innovative ways to make my products more eco-friendly. Whether using recycled materials, designing products with minimal waste, or incorporating renewable energy sources into my production process, I'm constantly exploring new ways to reduce my environmental impact without sacrificing quality or performance. Sustainability doesn't end once the product leaves my warehouse. I also think about the entire lifecycle of my products, from cradle to grave. That means considering the environmental impact of everything from transportation and distribution to end-of-life disposal. By designing durable, repairable, and recyclable products, I can minimize waste and maximize the lifespan of my products, ensuring that they have a positive impact on the planet for years to come.

Sustainable Supply Chain Management

Running a business has taught me that sustainability isn't just about the final product—it's about every step of the journey, including the supply chain. When I think about sustainable supply chain management, I'm considering the entire network of suppliers, manufacturers, distributors, and retailers that bring my products to life and get them into the hands of customers.

For me, supply chain sustainability starts with transparency. I believe in knowing exactly where my materials are coming from and how they are produced. That means working with suppliers who share my commitment to ethical labor practices, fair wages, and environmental stewardship. Whether it's sourcing organic cotton for my clothing line or using recycled materials for my packaging, I want to ensure that every link in the supply chain reflects my values.

However, sustainability isn't just about the materials—it's also about how those materials are transported and processed. That's why I prioritize reducing the carbon footprint of my supply chain wherever possible. Whether by choosing local suppliers to minimize transportation emissions or optimizing packaging to reduce waste, I'm always looking for ways to make my supply chain more sustainable without compromising efficiency or quality.

Supply chain sustainability isn't always easy. It requires collaboration, communication, and a willingness to challenge the status quo. But for me, it's worth it. By investing in a sustainable supply chain, I'm not just reducing my environmental impact—I'm also building stronger relationships with my suppliers, improving the resilience of my business, and creating a better world for future generations.

As a business owner committed to sustainability, I've learned that promoting these values among my suppliers and throughout the logistics and distribution process is key to achieving my goals. When it comes to working with suppliers, I approach it as a partnership built on shared values and mutual respect.

One strategy I've found effective is clearly communicating my sustainability expectations from the start. When I onboard new suppliers, I make it a point to discuss my company's commitment to ethical sourcing, environmentally friendly practices, and fair labor standards. By setting these expectations upfront, I ensure that we're on the same page and that they understand the importance of sustainability to my business.

Another strategy is to incentivize sustainable behavior. For example, I offer preferential treatment to suppliers who meet or exceed certain sustainability criteria. This could include offering longer-term contracts, paying a premium for eco-friendly materials, or providing recognition for outstanding sustainability efforts. By rewarding suppliers for their sustainability initiatives, I encourage them to prioritize these practices and create a competitive advantage for my business.

In terms of logistics and distribution, I believe in leading by example. I strive to implement ethical and sustainable practices at every stage of the process, from transportation to packaging. For instance, I prioritize eco-friendly shipping methods whenever possible, opting for modes of transport with lower carbon emissions and seeking out packaging materials that are recyclable or biodegradable.

Additionally, I actively seek opportunities to streamline the logistics process to minimize waste and optimize efficiency. This might involve consolidating shipments to reduce the number of trips or investing in technology that allows for real-time tracking and route optimization. By continuously evaluating and improving our logistics practices, I aim to minimize our environmental footprint while enhancing our operations' overall efficiency.

Overall, promoting sustainability among suppliers and implementing ethical practices in logistics and distribution are essential components of my business strategy. By working collaboratively with our partners and taking proactive steps to minimize our environmental impact, I believe we can create a more sustainable future for our business and the planet.

Engaging Stakeholders in Sustainability

In my business journey, I've recognized the pivotal role of stakeholder engagement in our sustainability efforts. It's not just about what we do as a company; it's about how we involve our employees, customers, and communities in our sustainability journey.

First, I've learned that engaging stakeholders is crucial because sustainability isn't a one-person job. It's a collective effort that requires input and commitment from everyone involved. That's why I've prioritized fostering a culture of sustainability within my organization, where employees feel empowered to contribute their ideas and efforts toward our sustainability goals.

One way I've achieved this is by promoting open communication and collaboration. I encourage my team members to share their thoughts and suggestions on improving our sustainability practices, whether it's through reducing waste in our operations or sourcing more sustainable materials for our products. By creating a safe space for dialogue and feedback, we can tap into the collective wisdom of our team and drive meaningful change together.

However, it's not just about internal stakeholders; it's also about engaging our customers and the communities we serve. I've found that involving them in our sustainability initiatives not only enhances our brand reputation but also fosters a sense of loyalty and trust. For example, we might seek our customers' input on how to make our products more sustainable or involve local communities in environmental cleanup efforts.

To encourage participation and feedback, I make sure to communicate our sustainability initiatives transparently and openly. Whether it's through newsletters, social media, or community events, I strive to keep stakeholders informed about our progress and actively solicit their input. I also make it a point to express gratitude for their contributions and recognize their efforts toward our shared sustainability goals.

Ultimately, engaging stakeholders in sustainability isn't just about ticking boxes; it's about building meaningful relationships and creating a shared purpose. By working together toward a common goal, we can make a real difference in creating a more sustainable future for our business and the world around us.

MEASURING AND REPORTING SUSTAINABILITY IMPACT

In my business, keeping track of our sustainability efforts isn't just about ticking boxes; it's about making sure we're making a real impact and holding ourselves accountable. That's why we've identified key performance indicators, or KPIs, to measure our sustainability impact.

These KPIs help us track our progress in areas like energy consumption, waste reduction, and carbon emissions. By setting clear targets and regularly monitoring our performance against these metrics, we can identify areas where we're excelling and areas where we need to improve.

But it's not just enough to measure our sustainability impact; we also believe in being transparent about our efforts. That's why we're committed to reporting our sustainability performance openly and honestly to our stakeholders, whether it's through annual sustainability reports, website updates, or social media posts.

Being transparent about our sustainability efforts builds trust with our stakeholders and holds us accountable for our actions. It shows that we're committed to positively impacting the environment and society and that we're not afraid to be held to a high standard.

Moreover, we don't just stop at measuring and reporting our sustainability impact; we also use this data to drive continuous improvement. By analyzing our performance data and identifying areas for enhancement, we can adjust our strategies and initiatives to become even more sustainable over time.

For example, if we notice that our energy consumption is higher than expected, we might explore ways to improve energy efficiency in our operations or invest in renewable energy sources. Likewise, if we find that our waste generation is increasing, we might look for ways to reduce waste through recycling programs or product redesign.

Measuring and reporting our sustainability impact isn't just a box to check; it's an essential part of our commitment to making a positive difference in the world. By setting clear KPIs, being transparent about our efforts, and using data to drive improvement, we're making our business more sustainable and contributing to a brighter future for generations to come.

ADDRESSING CHALLENGES AND OVERCOMING BARRIERS

I've encountered various challenges when it comes to implementing sustainable engagement practices. These hurdles aren't uncommon in the business world but require thoughtful strategies to overcome.

One common challenge is the initial cost associated with adopting sustainable practices. Whether investing in energy-efficient equipment or sourcing sustainable materials, there's often an upfront expense involved. As a business owner, balancing these costs with other priorities can be tricky, but it's essential to recognize the long-term benefits of sustainability. By focusing on the potential cost savings, improved brand reputation, and reduced environmental impact, I've found it easier to justify these investments to myself and my team.

Another challenge is navigating complex regulations and standards related to sustainability. With ever-changing legislation and industry standards, staying compliant can feel like navigating a maze. To address this challenge, I've prioritized staying informed about relevant regulations and seeking expert guidance when needed. By partnering with consultants or industry organizations, I've been able to ensure that my business remains compliant while also staying ahead of emerging trends and opportunities.

Additionally, resistance to change can be a significant barrier to implementing sustainable practices. Whether it's from employees, suppliers, or customers, not everyone may be on board with embracing sustainability. To overcome this resistance, I've focused on education and communication. By clearly explaining the rationale behind our sustainability initiatives and demonstrating the benefits, I've been able to garner more support and buy-in from stakeholders.

Despite these challenges, I've seen firsthand how businesses can successfully overcome barriers to sustainability. Many companies have made significant strides in their sustainability journey through innovative strategies and perseverance. For example, I've been inspired by case studies of companies implementing creative solutions to reduce waste, optimize resource usage, and engage stakeholders in meaningful ways.

These success stories prove that with determination and the right approach, businesses can overcome challenges and make meaningful progress toward sustainability. By learning from these examples and staying committed to our sustainability goals, I'm confident that my business can continue to thrive while positively impacting the planet and society.

CONCLUSION

As I wrap up this chapter on sustainable engagement, I can't help but reflect on the valuable insights we've covered. Throughout our discussion, we've explored the significance of sustainability in today's business landscape and how it's not just a trend but a crucial aspect of long-term success.

We started by understanding what sustainable engagement truly means and why it's essential for building lasting relationships with customers, employees, and communities. By embracing sustainability, businesses can reduce their environmental footprint and foster stakeholder trust and loyalty.

We then delved into practical strategies for building a sustainable brand, from incorporating sustainability into our brand identity to effectively communicating our efforts to customers. By aligning our business practices with sustainable values, we can differentiate ourselves in the market and attract like-minded customers who share our commitment to environmental and social responsibility.

Next, we explored the importance of sustainable product development and supply chain management. By sourcing materials responsibly, innovating in product design and packaging, and promoting sustainability among our suppliers, we can minimize our environmental impact and contribute to a more sustainable future.

Engaging stakeholders in sustainability initiatives was another key focus of our discussion. By collaborating with employees, customers, and communities, we can amplify our impact and create meaningful change. Encouraging participation and feedback ensures that our sustainability efforts are aligned with the needs and values of those we serve.

Throughout this chapter, we've also emphasized the importance of measuring and reporting on our sustainability impact. We can hold ourselves accountable and drive continuous improvement by identifying key performance indicators and reporting on our progress transparently.

As we look ahead, I'm excited to explore additional strategies for business sustainability and success in the chapters to come. From renewable energy solutions to circular economy practices, businesses have countless opportunities to make a positive impact while driving growth and innovation.

In conclusion, sustainable engagement isn't just a responsibility; it's a tremendous opportunity for businesses to thrive in a rapidly changing world. By prioritizing sustainability in our business practices, we can create value for both our business and society as a whole.

9

METRICS AND MEASUREMENT

A clear understanding of our performance is crucial in the fast-paced business world. It's like navigating a ship—we need reliable instruments to steer us in the right direction. That's where metrics and measurement come into play. This chapter will explore the world of key performance indicators, or KPIs, which serve as our compass in the vast sea of business operations.

KPIs are like signposts on the road to success. They tell us how well we're doing in various aspects of our business, whether it's financial health, operational efficiency, customer satisfaction, or employee engagement. We can make informed decisions and steer our business toward its goals by paying attention to these indicators.

Throughout this chapter, we'll delve into the different types of KPIs and how they apply to different areas of our business. We'll explore financial metrics, such as revenue and profit margins, which help us understand the financial health of our company. Operational metrics, like production efficiency and cycle time, will show us how smoothly our operations are running. Customer-related metrics, such as satisfaction and retention rates, will show how well we serve our customers. And employee-related metrics, like satisfaction and productivity, will give us insight into the strength of our team.

By the end of this chapter, you'll have a solid understanding of how to identify, track, and interpret KPIs to drive your business forward. So, let's dive in and uncover the power of metrics and measurement in achieving business success.

UNDERSTANDING KEY PERFORMANCE INDICATORS (KPIS)

Key Performance Indicators, or KPIs, are the heartbeat of any successful business. They're like the vital signs a doctor checks to assess a patient's health. These indicators clearly show how well our business is performing in various areas.

Think of KPIs as our business's report card. They tell us if we're hitting our targets, meeting our goals, and staying on track. Whether it's sales numbers, customer satisfaction scores, or production efficiency rates, KPIs give us a measurable way to gauge our progress.

KPIs aren't just numbers on a spreadsheet but strategic tools guiding our decision-making. By focusing on the right KPIs, we can identify strengths, pinpoint weaknesses, and make informed adjustments to improve our performance.

For instance, if our customer satisfaction KPIs show a decline, it's a signal that we need to pay more attention to our customers' needs and preferences. If our sales KPIs are stagnant, it may be time to reassess our marketing strategies or product offerings.

Understanding KPIs isn't just about knowing what they are; it's about knowing how to use them effectively. It's about selecting the right KPIs that align with our business objectives and regularly monitoring them to track our progress. Understanding the different types of Key Performance Indicators, or KPIs, is like having a toolbox filled with various tools for different jobs. Each type serves a unique purpose in helping us assess and improve different aspects of our business. First, there are financial KPIs. These are like our financial GPS, guiding us on the path to profitability. They include metrics like revenue, profit margins, and cash flow. By tracking financial KPIs, we can see if our business is making money, where it's coming from, and where it's going.

Operational KPIs are like the gears that keep our business running smoothly. They measure things like production efficiency, inventory turnover, and delivery times. These KPIs help us identify bottlenecks, streamline processes, and optimize our operations for maximum efficiency.

Next, we have customer-related KPIs. These are like our customer satisfaction compass, showing how well we meet our customers' needs and expectations. Customer-related KPIs include metrics like customer satisfaction scores, Net Promoter Score (NPS), and customer retention rates. By tracking these KPIs, we can ensure that our customers are happy and loyal, which ultimately drives business growth.

Last but not least, we have employee-related KPIs. These are like our team performance indicators, measuring the effectiveness and productivity of our workforce. Employee-related KPIs include metrics like employee turnover rates, absenteeism, and productivity levels. By tracking these KPIs, we can identify areas for improvement, provide targeted training and support, and create a positive work environment that fosters employee engagement and satisfaction.

When it comes to selecting KPIs for our business, relevance and actionability are key. We want to choose KPIs directly tied to our business goals and objectives, providing actionable insights we can use to drive meaningful change. By selecting the right mix of KPIs from each category, we can gain a holistic view of our business performance and make informed decisions to drive success.

FINANCIAL METRICS

Understanding financial metrics is crucial for any business owner, including myself. These metrics act as our financial compass, guiding us through the business's ups and downs.

Firstly, let's talk about revenue. Revenue is like the lifeblood of our business—it's the money coming in from sales of our products or services. Tracking our revenue helps us understand how much money we're making and whether our sales efforts are paying off.

Next up, we have profit margins. Profit margins tell us how much money we're making after subtracting the costs associated with producing our goods or services. It's like looking at the bottom line to see how much profit we're pocketing. Keeping an eye on our profit margins helps us ensure that our business is sustainable and profitable in the long run.

Then, there's cash flow. Cash flow is like the rhythm of our business—it's the movement of cash in and out of our company. Positive cash flow means we're bringing in more money than we're spending, while negative cash flow signals trouble ahead. Monitoring our cash flow helps us manage our finances effectively, ensuring we can cover expenses and invest in growth opportunities when needed.

Beyond these essentials, there are other financial metrics to consider, like return on investment (ROI), gross margin, and debt-to-equity ratio. Each of these metrics provides valuable insights into different aspects of our financial health, helping us make informed decisions to drive business growth.

As a business owner, having a solid grasp of these financial metrics is essential for making strategic decisions and steering our business toward success. By regularly monitoring and analyzing our financial performance, we can identify areas for improvement, seize opportunities for growth, and navigate challenges with confidence.

Understanding financial ratios is like having a toolkit for dissecting my business's performance. These ratios allow me to dig deeper into my financial data and gain insights into different aspects of my company's health.

One important set of ratios is liquidity ratios. These ratios help me understand my company's ability to meet short-term financial obligations without jeopardizing its long-term stability. For example, the current ratio compares current assets to current liabilities, giving me a snapshot of my company's liquidity position. If this ratio is too low, it could signal potential cash flow problems in the near future.

Profitability ratios, on the other hand, shed light on how effectively my business is generating profits from its operations. For instance, the gross profit margin ratio compares gross profit to total revenue, showing me the percentage of revenue that's left after accounting for the cost of goods sold. By tracking this ratio over time, I can gauge whether my business is becoming more or less efficient in generating profits.

Solvency ratios are yet another crucial category of financial ratios. These ratios help me assess my company's long-term financial health and its ability to meet its debt obligations. For example, the debt-to-equity ratio compares total debt to total equity, indicating the proportion of financing that comes from debt versus equity. A high debt-to-equity ratio may signal that my company is relying too heavily on debt to finance its operations, potentially putting it at risk in the event of economic downturns.

Now, let's talk about how I apply these financial metrics in real-world decision-making. Take, for example, a scenario where I'm considering expanding my business by opening a new location. Before making this decision, I would analyze various financial metrics, including liquidity ratios to ensure I have enough cash on hand to fund the expansion, profitability ratios to assess the potential return on investment, and solvency ratios to ensure the expansion won't strain my company's financial resources.

By using these financial ratios as my compass, I can make more informed decisions that align with my business goals and financial objectives. By learning from case studies of other businesses that have successfully applied these metrics, I can gain valuable insights and avoid common pitfalls along the way. Integrating financial ratios into my decision-making process ultimately empowers me to steer my business toward sustainable growth and long-term success.

Operational Metrics

Operational metrics are the heartbeat of my business. They're like the vital signs that tell me how efficiently my operations are running and where there might be room for improvement.

Take production efficiency, for example. This metric gives me insight into how well my resources are utilized to produce goods or deliver services. By tracking metrics like the number of units produced per hour or the percentage of time machinery is operational, I can identify bottlenecks in my production process and make adjustments to streamline operations.

Quality metrics are another essential aspect of my operational toolkit. These metrics help me gauge the level of quality of my products or services and ensure that they meet or exceed customer expectations. For instance, tracking metrics like defect rates or customer complaints allows me to pinpoint areas where quality issues may arise and take corrective action to maintain high standards.

Cycle time is yet another critical operational metric. It measures the time it takes to complete a specific task or process from start to finish. By analyzing cycle times for different operations within my business, I can identify areas where processes are taking longer than they should and implement strategies to improve efficiency and reduce waste.

Now, let's talk about how I implement these operational metrics. Suppose I notice that my production efficiency has been declining steadily over the past few months. Upon closer inspection, I discovered that one of my manufacturing machines frequently breaks down, causing costly production delays.

Armed with this insight, I decided to invest in preventive maintenance for the machine to reduce the frequency of breakdowns and minimize downtime. Additionally, I implement a regular inspection schedule to catch any potential issues early on and address them before they escalate.

By monitoring operational metrics like production efficiency, quality, and cycle time, I can proactively identify and address issues that may be hindering my business's performance. This allows me to continuously optimize my operations, deliver high-quality products or services to my customers, and stay ahead of the competition.

Tracking operational metrics is like having a compass for my business operations. It guides me on the path to improvement and optimization, helping me navigate challenges and seize opportunities along the way.

One of the key reasons why I prioritize tracking operational metrics is for process improvement. These metrics provide me with valuable insights into how well my business processes are performing and where there may be opportunities for enhancement. By regularly monitoring metrics like production efficiency, quality, and cycle time, I can identify inefficiencies or bottlenecks in my operations and take targeted actions to streamline processes.

For instance, let's say I run a manufacturing company that produces furniture. I can pinpoint areas where improvements can be made by tracking operational metrics, such as the time it takes to complete each production step and the percentage of defective products. Suppose I notice that a particular production stage is taking longer than expected or that the defect rate is higher than desired. In that case, I can investigate the root causes and implement changes to optimize the process.

However, operational metrics aren't just limited to manufacturing businesses. They're applicable across various industries, from retail to healthcare to hospitality. For example, in retail, metrics like inventory turnover and customer wait time can provide valuable insights into store performance and customer satisfaction. In healthcare, metrics such as patient wait times and hospital readmission rates are crucial for ensuring efficient and effective care delivery.

The impact of operational metrics on business performance cannot be overstated. By tracking and analyzing these metrics, I can make data-driven decisions that drive efficiency, improve quality, and, ultimately, enhance the overall performance of my business. Whether it's reducing production costs, increasing customer satisfaction, or improving patient outcomes, operational metrics play a vital role in driving success across industries.

Customer-Related Metrics

Understanding my customers is at the heart of my business strategy. That's why I pay close attention to customer-related metrics—they give me valuable insights into how well I'm meeting their needs and how I can improve their experience with my brand.

Customer-related metrics cover a wide range of aspects, from customer satisfaction to retention and acquisition costs. These metrics help me gauge the health of my customer relationships and identify areas where I can improve.

For instance, tracking customer satisfaction allows me to understand how happy my customers are with my products or services. By regularly surveying them or analyzing feedback, I can pinpoint areas where I excel and need to improve. If I notice a dip in satisfaction, I can take swift action to address any issues and ensure my customers remain happy and loyal.

Customer retention is another crucial metric for me. It tells me how successful I am at keeping customers coming back for more. By analyzing retention rates, I can identify patterns and trends that may indicate areas for improvement. For example, if I notice a drop in retention among a certain demographic, I can tailor my marketing efforts to better appeal to their needs and preferences.

Acquisition cost is equally important. It tells me how much it costs to acquire a new customer, which is essential for ensuring my marketing efforts are cost-effective. By tracking this metric, I can identify the most efficient channels for acquiring new customers and allocate my resources accordingly.

But it's not just about tracking these metrics—it's also about using them to drive action and improvement. For example, suppose I notice that my customer acquisition cost is high compared to the industry average. In that case, I might explore ways to improve my targeting or optimize my ad campaigns to reduce costs.

Case studies are incredibly helpful in this regard. They provide real-world examples of how other businesses have used customer-related metrics to drive growth and loyalty. By studying these cases, I can gain valuable insights and inspiration for my business.

Overall, customer-related metrics are invaluable tools for me as a business owner. They help me understand my customers better, identify areas for improvement, and ultimately, drive growth and loyalty for my business.

EMPLOYEE-RELATED METRICS

I've realized that my employees are my most valuable asset in my business. That's why I pay close attention to employee-related metrics—they give me insights into how satisfied my team is, how productive they are, and, ultimately, how engaged they are with their work.

Employee-related metrics cover a range of factors, from employee satisfaction to turnover rate and productivity. These metrics help me understand the health of my workforce and identify areas where I can make improvements to create a more positive and productive workplace.

Employee satisfaction is crucial because happy employees are more likely to be engaged and productive. By regularly surveying my team or soliciting feedback, I can gauge their satisfaction with their roles, work environment, and the company. If I notice any issues, I can address them proactively to ensure my team remains motivated and fulfilled in their jobs.

The turnover rate is another important metric for me. High turnover can be costly and disrupt my business, so I prioritize tracking this metric closely. If I notice a higher-than-average turnover rate, it's a red flag that something may be amiss, whether it's poor management, lack of growth opportunities, or cultural issues. I can reduce turnover and retain top talent by addressing these issues promptly.

Productivity is equally important. It tells me how efficiently my team works and how effectively they deliver results. By tracking productivity metrics, such as output per employee or project completion rates, I can identify areas where my team may need additional support or resources to perform at their best.

But it's not just about tracking these metrics—it's also about fostering a positive workplace culture that encourages engagement and productivity. This means creating an environment where employees feel valued, supported, and empowered to do their best work.

Best practices for measuring and fostering a positive workplace culture include regular check-ins with employees, providing opportunities for growth and development, and recognizing and rewarding achievements. By prioritizing employee well-being and investing in their professional development, I can create a workplace where my team feels motivated, engaged, and fulfilled.

Ultimately, employee-related metrics are essential for me as a business owner because they help me understand and support my team effectively. By prioritizing employee satisfaction, minimizing turnover, and maximizing productivity, I can create a positive and productive workplace culture that drives success for my business.

DATA COLLECTION AND ANALYSIS

Understanding data is crucial for making informed decisions and driving success in my business. That's why I rely on various methods to collect and analyze data related to our key performance indicators (KPIs).

One method we use is surveys. Surveys allow us to gather direct feedback from customers, employees, or other stakeholders, helping us understand their needs, preferences, and satisfaction levels. We also leverage analytics tools like Google Analytics or CRM systems to track website traffic, sales performance, and other relevant metrics. These tools provide us with valuable data points that we can use to measure our progress against our goals.

Performance reports are another essential tool in our data collection arsenal. These reports compile data from various sources, showing how well we perform across different business areas. Whether it's sales figures, customer retention rates, or operational efficiency metrics, performance reports give us a comprehensive view of our business's health.

Once we've collected the data, we will analyze and interpret it to gain actionable insights. We use techniques like trend analysis, correlation analysis, and benchmarking to identify patterns, relationships, and areas for improvement. For example, if we notice a decline in customer satisfaction scores, we'll investigate the possible causes and develop strategies to address them.

Data visualization plays a crucial role in our analysis process. We can communicate trends and patterns more effectively by presenting KPI data in visually appealing and easy-to-understand formats, such as charts, graphs, or dashboards. This allows us to share insights with stakeholders across the organization and drive alignment toward common goals.

Overall, data collection and analysis are integral parts of our business operations. By leveraging various methods and techniques, we can gather, interpret, and visualize data to make informed decisions and drive continuous improvement.

IMPLEMENTING A MEASUREMENT FRAMEWORK

Setting up a solid measurement framework in my business is key to tracking our progress and ensuring we're on the right path. Developing this framework involves a few key steps.

First, we identify our business objectives. We want to achieve these big-picture goals, like increasing sales, improving customer satisfaction, or reducing operational costs. Once we have a clear understanding of our objectives, we can start to break them down into smaller, measurable targets.

Next, we select the key performance indicators (KPIs) that will help us track our progress toward these objectives. These might include metrics like revenue growth, customer retention rates, or employee productivity. Choosing KPIs that are closely aligned with our business goals and that we can realistically measure and influence is important.

With our KPIs identified, we integrate them into our strategic planning and decision-making processes. This means that we use them to inform our strategies and tactics and regularly review them to see if we're on track. For example, if our goal is to increase customer satisfaction, we might use feedback surveys and Net Promoter Score (NPS) as KPIs to gauge how well we're meeting customer needs.

Finally, we understand that our business environment is constantly changing, so we make sure to continuously monitor and adjust our KPIs as needed. This might involve refining our metrics, adding new ones, or even removing ones that are no longer relevant. By staying agile and responsive, we can ensure that our measurement framework remains effective in guiding our business toward success.

Challenges and Pitfalls in Metrics and Measurement

In my experience, navigating the world of metrics and measurement isn't always smooth sailing. There are often challenges and pitfalls along the way that can trip up even the most well-intentioned business owner.

One of the most common challenges is selecting the right KPIs. With so many metrics to choose from, it can be overwhelming to decide which ones will truly measure our progress toward our goals. Sometimes, we might focus on metrics that are easy to measure but don't tell us much about our business performance. Other times, we might choose too broad or too narrow metrics, making it difficult to gauge our success accurately.

Another challenge is ensuring data accuracy and reliability. In today's data-driven world, it's easy to collect massive amounts of data, but not all of it is useful or accurate. We must diligently collect data from reliable sources and ensure it's clean and error-free. Otherwise, we risk making decisions based on faulty information, which can lead us astray.

Implementing KPIs effectively also requires buy-in from all levels of the organization. Suppose our employees don't understand the importance of the metrics we're tracking or don't have the tools and resources to collect and analyze data effectively. In that case, our measurement efforts will fall flat. It's crucial to communicate clearly with our team about why certain metrics matter and how they can contribute to our overall success.

Despite these challenges, there are strategies we can employ to overcome them. One approach is to start small and gradually expand our measurement efforts over time. By focusing on a few key metrics initially, we can gain confidence in our measurement capabilities and gradually add more as we grow more comfortable.

Additionally, it's essential to continually evaluate and adjust our measurement approach as needed. If certain KPIs aren't providing valuable insights or are too difficult to track, we shouldn't be afraid to pivot and try something new. Flexibility and adaptability are key traits of successful measurement strategies.

Ultimately, learning from both our successes and failures is essential in the world of metrics and measurement. By studying case studies and real-life examples of KPI implementation, we can glean valuable lessons that will help us refine our approach and drive our business forward.

CONCLUSION

As I reflect on the journey through the realm of metrics and measurement, I'm struck by the profound impact these tools have on shaping the course of my business. We've covered a lot of ground, diving into the intricacies of key performance indicators (KPIs), exploring various types of metrics, and learning how to implement them effectively.

Throughout this chapter, I've come to appreciate the pivotal role that metrics and measurement play in driving business performance. They serve as our compass, guiding us toward our goals and illuminating the path to success. Whether it's tracking financial health, optimizing operations, understanding our customers, or engaging our employees, metrics provide invaluable insights that inform our decision-making and drive continuous improvement.

As I look ahead, I'm reminded of the importance of embracing metrics and measurement as integral components of our business strategy. By harnessing the power of data-driven insights, we can better understand our strengths and weaknesses, identify areas for growth, and make informed decisions that propel our business forward.

In the next chapters, we'll continue exploring additional tools and strategies for business improvement. From harnessing the power of technology to fostering innovation and creativity, there's always more to learn and discover on the journey toward business excellence. So, let's stay curious, stay open-minded, and continue to embrace the power of metrics and measurement as we chart the course toward success.

10

CONCLUSION

RECAP OF KEY THEMES

As I reflect on the journey we've taken together in this book, it's essential to revisit some of the core themes and insights we've uncovered along the way. Throughout our exploration, we've delved into many concepts to enhance our understanding of business management and strategy.

One of the central themes that emerged is the importance of adaptability in the ever-evolving landscape of business. We've discussed how businesses must be agile and responsive to changes in the market, technology, and consumer preferences to remain competitive. This adaptability encompasses everything from embracing new technologies to pivoting business models when necessary.

Additionally, we've emphasized the significance of customer-centricity in driving business success. By prioritizing the needs and preferences of our customers, we can build stronger relationships, enhance brand loyalty, and drive sustainable growth. This customer-centric approach permeates every aspect of business operations, from product development to marketing strategies.

Furthermore, we've explored the vital role of innovation in driving business growth and differentiation. Whether it's through product innovation, process improvement, or disruptive business models, innovation is essential for staying ahead of the curve and creating value for customers.

As we journeyed through this book's various topics and chapters, we've uncovered valuable insights and practical strategies that can be applied to real-world business scenarios. From marketing tactics to financial management techniques, each chapter has offered actionable takeaways aimed at helping businesses thrive in today's dynamic environment.

REFLECTION ON PERSONAL GROWTH

Looking back on the journey through this book, I find myself reflecting on the personal growth and insights gained along the way. Each chapter has offered a unique lens through which to view the complex world of business management, providing valuable lessons that have shaped my perspective.

One of the most significant insights I've gained is the importance of adaptability and resilience in the face of challenges. The ever-changing nature of the business landscape demands flexibility and the ability to pivot strategies when necessary. Through our exploration of different topics, I've learned to embrace change as an opportunity for growth rather than a setback.

Another valuable lesson I've learned is the power of customer-centricity in driving business success. By placing the needs and preferences of our customers at the forefront of decision-making, we can build stronger relationships and create more value for our target audience. This mindset shift has profoundly influenced how I approach marketing and product development strategies.

Furthermore, delving into the intricacies of financial management has provided me with a deeper understanding of the importance of sound financial practices in sustaining and growing a business. From managing cash flow to analyzing profitability ratios, I've gained practical skills that will serve me well in navigating the financial aspects of entrepreneurship.

The journey through this book has been a transformative experience filled with valuable insights and practical wisdom. As I continue to apply these lessons in my business endeavors, I am confident that they will continue to shape my growth and success in the dynamic world of business management.

APPLICATION TO BUSINESS PRACTICES

As I reflect on how to apply the insights gleaned from this journey to my business practices, I find myself drawn to the practical strategies and tactics that can be readily implemented to drive positive change. One of the key takeaways from our exploration is the importance of adaptability and agility in responding to market dynamics. Armed with this understanding, I am motivated to instill a culture of innovation within my organization, encouraging my team to embrace change and explore new growth opportunities.

Furthermore, our discussion on customer-centricity has underscored the significance of understanding and meeting the needs of our target audience. I plan to prioritize customer feedback and insights in shaping our product development and marketing strategies. By fostering closer relationships with our customers and listening attentively to their concerns, we can ensure that our offerings remain relevant and impactful.

Additionally, the insights gained from exploring financial management principles have highlighted the importance of sound fiscal stewardship in sustaining business growth. Armed with this knowledge, I am committed to implementing robust financial practices within my organization, from meticulous budgeting to prudent investment decisions. Maintaining a firm grasp on our financial health can position us for long-term success and resilience amid economic uncertainties.

In integrating these key learnings into our daily business operations, I recognize the importance of fostering a culture of continuous improvement and learning. By encouraging open communication and collaboration across all levels of the organization, we can harness the collective wisdom of our team to drive innovation and excellence. By applying these practical tips and strategies, I am confident that we can chart a course toward sustained growth and success in the competitive business landscape.

LOOKING FORWARD

As I gaze toward the horizon of business management, I can't help but wonder about the future trends and developments that lie ahead. The landscape of commerce is ever-evolving, shaped by technological advancements, shifting consumer behaviors, and global economic forces. In this dynamic environment, staying ahead of the curve and anticipating emerging trends that could impact our business is essential.

One trend I foresee gaining momentum is the increasing emphasis on sustainability and social responsibility. As consumers become more environmentally conscious, businesses will need to adapt their practices to meet this growing demand for eco-friendly products and ethical sourcing. Embracing sustainability aligns with our moral values and presents opportunities for innovation and differentiation in the market.

Another trend on the horizon is the continued rise of digitalization and data-driven decision-making. With the proliferation of digital technologies, businesses are generating vast amounts of data that can be leveraged to gain valuable insights into consumer preferences, market trends, and operational efficiency. As we move forward, investing in robust data analytics capabilities will be crucial for staying competitive and agile in an increasingly data-driven world.

Furthermore, I believe that a renewed focus on agility and resilience will characterize the future of business management. The COVID-19 pandemic has underscored the importance of adaptability and the ability to pivot quickly in response to unexpected disruptions. As businesses move forward, they must build flexibility into their operations, enabling them to navigate uncertain times with confidence and resilience.

There are countless opportunities for continued learning and professional development. Whether honing our leadership skills, deepening our understanding of emerging technologies, or staying abreast of industry trends, there's always room to grow and evolve as business leaders. By embracing a mindset of lifelong learning and remaining open to new ideas and perspectives, we can position ourselves for success in the ever-changing landscape of business management.

GRATITUDE AND ACKNOWLEDGMENTS

As I reflect on the journey we've taken together in exploring the intricacies of business management, I am filled with a profound sense of gratitude for all those who have supported and contributed to our collective growth and success.

First, I want to express my heartfelt appreciation to my mentors, whose guidance and wisdom have been invaluable throughout this journey. Their insights and advice have served as guiding lights, illuminating the path forward and helping me navigate the challenges and opportunities of business management with confidence and clarity.

I am also deeply grateful to my colleagues and peers, whose collaboration and camaraderie have immeasurably enriched the learning experience. Through our shared discussions, debates, and brainstorming sessions, we have fostered a culture of innovation and creativity, pushing the boundaries of what's possible and inspiring one another to strive for excellence. Additionally, I want to extend my thanks to the countless resources and materials that have helped shape our understanding of business management. From insightful books and articles to thought-provoking podcasts and webinars, these resources have provided us with a wealth of knowledge and inspiration, empowering us to continuously learn and grow as business leaders.

Finally, I am grateful to you, the reader, for joining me on this journey. Your curiosity, engagement, and willingness to explore new ideas have driven our collective pursuit of knowledge and understanding. Together, we have embarked on a journey of discovery, seeking to unlock the secrets of business management and chart a course toward greater success and fulfillment.

As we bring this chapter to a close, I want to express my deepest gratitude to every one of you. Your support, encouragement, and friendship have been the fuel that has propelled us forward, and for that, I am truly thankful.

FINAL THOUGHTS

As I conclude our journey through the world of business management, I'm reminded of the importance of continuous learning and improvement. In the dynamic landscape of business, staying stagnant is not an option. We must always evolve, adapt to changes, and seek new growth opportunities.

Throughout this book, we've explored various strategies, tactics, and principles aimed at enhancing our understanding and effectiveness as business owners. From developing sustainable engagement practices to measuring and analyzing key performance indicators, each chapter has offered valuable insights into different facets of business management.

But knowledge alone is not enough. It's what we do with that knowledge that truly matters. As we close this chapter, I want to encourage you, the reader, to take action. Apply the lessons learned, experiment with new ideas, and embrace the journey of continuous improvement.

Success in business is not always linear. There will be challenges and setbacks along the way. However, we can overcome these obstacles through perseverance and resilience and forge our paths to success.

As you embark on your entrepreneurial journey, remember that learning is a lifelong pursuit. Embrace curiosity, seek new opportunities for growth, and never stop striving to be the best version of yourself.

With that, I wish you all the best in your endeavors. May you find fulfillment, prosperity, and success in all your future endeavors.

Work Less and Make More Money Than Ever Before

Take your business to the next level
with a fresh perspective.

These insights show you exactly how to break
through plateaus and achieve big profits.

Go beyond your expectations and
see what's possible for your business.

jetlaunch.link/sab2